The Spider Strategy

Six Steps to Outstanding

Marcella McCarthy

BLOOMSBURY

LONDON · NEW DELHI · NEW YORK · SYDNEY

Bloomsbury Education
An imprint of Bloomsbury Publishing Plc

50 Bedford Square
London
WC1B 3DP
UK

1385 Broadway
New York
NY 10018
USA

www.bloomsbury.com

Bloomsbury is a registered trade mark of Bloomsbury Publishing Plc

Published 2014

British Library Cataloguing-in-Publication Data
A catalogue record for this book is available from the British Library.

ISBN:
PB: 9781472908643
ePub: 9781472908667
ePDF: 9781472908650

Library of Congress Cataloging-in-Publication Data
A catalog record for this book is available from the Library of Congress.

10 9 8 7 6 5 4 3 2 1

Typeset by Newgen Knowledge Works (P) Ltd., Chennai, India
Printed by CPI Group (UK) Ltd, Croydon, CR0 4YY

This book is produced using paper that is made from wood grown in
managed, sustainable forests. It is natural, renewable and recyclable.
The logging and manufacturing processes conform to the environmental
regulations of the country of origin.

To view more of our titles please visit www.bloomsbury.com

To John, Thea, and Felix
who, between them, have taught me
everything that is worth knowing.

Also available from Bloomsbury Education:

Getting the Buggers to Behave by Sue Cowley

How to Survive your First Year in Teaching by Sue Cowley

Pimp Your Lesson! by Isabella Wallace and Leah Kirkman

100 Ideas for Secondary Teachers: Gifted and Talented by John Senior

100 Ideas for Secondary Teachers: Outstanding English Lessons by Angella Cooze and Mary Myatt

100 Ideas for Secondary Teachers: Outstanding Mathematics Lessons by Mike Ollerton

100 Ideas for Secondary Teachers: Outstanding Lessons by Ross Morrison McGill

Contents

Acknowledgements

I would like to thank my students, who are ultimately responsible for all these strategies, and those who have taught me, advised me, and with whom I have been fortunate enough to work. I am indebted to Do Neville, who first inspired me to become a teacher, Gabrielle Durrant and Dominique Neville for their constant support and advice and Juliette Toye and Richard Watt for many lively discussions about teaching.

Many thanks to my colleagues at the SSAT and NATE for their confidence in and input into my first presentations of the Spider Strategy ideas. I would like to thank Stefan Hawlin, Tim Brighouse, David Brown, Phil Beadle, Ian Thompson, Niall McWilliams, and Dylan Wiliams for their wise thoughts and motivating conversations about teaching and learning.

I am deeply grateful to have been able to work with the dedicated and committed teachers of The Cherwell School, The Oxford Academy and Oxford City Learning, who remind me daily why I went into teaching. And for their encouragement during the writing of this book. Mal Dolan, Carmel McNamara, and Paul Slater deserve special praise for so often showing me—and their lucky students—what outstanding teaching should really look like.

Especial thanks are due to Gaynor Pollard, probably the very first librarian to order this book.

Introduction

As a veteran skipper of introductions, turner to the last page of the mystery, Wikipedia film cheat, and assembler of flat-pack furniture without looking at the pictures, I would like to apologise for this introduction and free you (should you feel any obligation) from reading it as a matter of narrative convention. Those who neither need nor care for an introduction will already be on page 75 in any case, so perhaps the permission is superfluous. Thank you, if you're still with me, for politely reading this far.

Teaching outstanding lessons

The four gradings of OFSTED—Outstanding (1), Good (2), Requires Improvement(3), and Inadequate (4)— were re-labelled in 2012, thus clearing up an issue that has troubled me ever since I read in the OFSTED report of a local primary: 'unfortunately, attendance is satisfactory'. This change has, however, accentuated a shift towards the top end of the criteria, reminiscent of the old joke that it is a scandal that 50% of schools are below average. With the re-labelling of the grading formerly known as 'satisfactory', 'good' has become the new default status for schools and teachers to chase (as if you require improvement you are clearly *not* satisfactory), and the pressure on teachers to be 'outstanding' has increased, this despite the fact that OFSTED is no longer labelling individual teachers or individual lessons with grades in inspections.

I like being called 'outstanding' or being told that my lessons are that way inclined, but it's a problematic judgement. Outstanding lessons don't have to be perfect. There are classes and situations where I think that the teacher is being pretty outstanding by just going into the room and staying there, schools with outstanding results where the teaching does not seem consistently better than elsewhere. In any scheme of work or run of lessons there may be some that will turn out less well than expected, because of a variety of factors—a wasp in the classroom, say, or a heavy snowfall closing the school mid-lesson. Any teacher who says that all her lessons are outstanding is either a big fibber, or the most non-reflective practitioner in existence. It is a mark, for me, of the excellent teacher that he is rarely satisfied with his lessons— always thinking of how they could be improved, always convinced that he could have done it better.

I'd like to distinguish this book by stating now that it is not going to provide you with something that will make every lesson you teach pure spun gold. What I can promise is that it will show you how to create a structure for your lessons that will make it easier to plan, easier to monitor what you're doing, and allow your inner outstanding teacher to flourish.

Know where you're going

It seems obvious, doesn't it—but many teachers teach lessons that they know will be observed as 'one-off' lessons. Everybody seems to have a story to tell of the slack Head of Department who nonetheless manages to teach perfectly during an SLT observation, or the teacher with the one outstanding lesson that is brought out, like a tarnished but still glittery Christmas tree, just for OFSTED. I have often witnessed teachers 'pull it out of the bag' for an observation, and been able to tell (from the faces of the students, if nothing else) that this is not what usually happens in their day-to-day teaching. Such lessons do nothing for school improvement. The teacher who stays up all night before an inspection to make it all perfect in this way is setting herself an impossible goal, and one which she cannot realistically reproduce in her day-to-day work. Creating something wonderful for an observation is only useful if:

A. It is going to be immediately embedded into a scheme of work for that class, or another class (or several classes, if it goes really well)

B. It is directly relevant to the scheme of work you are currently teaching

C. It actually helps the students to make progress.

When you teach an excellent lesson, it should be excellent because it fits into the pattern of the overall scheme of work. Otherwise, where are those students going to be tomorrow—looking wistfully after the OFSTED inspector as they bid farewell to the last exciting lesson they will see until next inspection time? To be a truly outstanding teacher, you need to embed strategies into your teaching so that students are *used* to working hard, *used* to challenge. Observations should become less stressful because they will be just that—observations of what you are doing, not tests.

Observation stress

No profession is currently as measured and evaluated as teaching, and there are few professions where so many challenges are faced on a daily basis. Most secondary teachers are responsible for hundreds of students, and have to evaluate and monitor their progress, as well as control their behaviour, over the course of at least a year. They have to be able to deal with physical disabilities and their impact on a child's learning on a daily basis. New guidelines establish that teachers are responsible for teaching their students social skills and moral awareness, and for consolidating literacy and numeracy as well as their chosen subject.

Teachers have to be experts in developing students with all kinds of special educational needs, coping with those who have emotional and behavioural problems, assisting the dyslexic or the child with a low reading level while also stretching those who are gifted and talented. They have to be able to negotiate the tangled streams of adolescence, working through friendship group problems, low self-esteem and bullying (for both perpetrator and bullied), creating a positive classroom dynamic from what may be a troubled group of children, all alongside their primary goal of transmitting knowledge about a particular subject area. Then when they're watched, 20 minutes' experience of a single group can form a judgement that follows them through their professional career.

Think about it for a moment. Imagine if doctors had to produce visible improvement in the health of a whole ward of patients over 20 minutes; if lawyers had to demonstrate measureable success in all the cases they had worked on over a year in 20 minutes; if bankers had to show sustained improvement in 30 different stock prices over a given 20 minutes. It becomes less surprising, on reflection, that teaching is apparently the most stressful occupation in Britain.

At a time when OFSTED is much in the news—and increased monitoring of teachers is also in the news—teachers are making a big mistake if they start to play what Paul Dix describes as 'the inspection game', so focused on potential observers in the classroom that the lesson turns into a performance, filled with changing activities, even though OFSTED now explicitly warn against such a strategy. This impressive, slick 'performance'-based culture results in teachers desperately trying to second-guess what will impress OFSTED, their managers, or a casual visitor, causing a great deal of stress, and taking teacher attention away from the real focus of the classroom—the students. In such circumstances, it is not surprising that there are relatively few outstanding lessons; it is astonishing that there are any at all.

The Spider Strategy

No teacher really needs an observer to tell them when they have taught a less-than-perfect lesson. In fact most teachers I know tend towards the morbidly self-critical, endlessly going over and over what they could have said or done to prevent Angelica telling the inspector to get the f*** out of her face, or Kyle throwing a paper plane across the room as the head entered. Sometimes such self-analysis is fruitful, and sometimes it is not, but ultimately, like some warrior hero of olden times, you just have to put the perceived disaster behind you and stride on into the golden future lesson that lies perhaps only a few minutes ahead, full of life and promise. The Spider Strategy was designed for that moment as you move on to that next lesson, something that will act as a quick checklist when you reflect on your plans.

Teaching an outstanding observed lesson does not have to mean masses of extra preparation and planning, for in this time of no-notice inspections, who can realistically do this? It needs to be authentic— because otherwise every student in your class will give away that you don't usually do this—and it needs to be a structure that you feel comfortable with. Spider Strategy contains everything that I think you need to have in an excellent lesson, everything you need to have in an excellent scheme of work, everything you need to have in a happy classroom—but most importantly, it is a framework for your own creativity and your own ideas; a reminder reduced to six key ideas around which you can structure your individual excellence as you open that door and walk into the next, outstanding, lesson.

The six key ideas form the six chapters of this book: Surprise, Purpose, Investigation, Differentiation, Evaluation and Record and Reflect. As well as advice for how to plan and implement these areas into your lessons there are some 'get weaving' boxes which provide extra teaching tips and activities to help you implement the Spider Strategy.

Join the conversation on Twitter and see how other teachers are using these ideas: #SpiderStrategy

---

1

Surprise: Learning by Stealth

Life, Friends, is boring. We must not say so.
(John Berryman *Dream Songs*)

> **What is the difference between a teacher and a train driver?**
> **Think about it, and I'll tell you my answer when you've given me**
> **five possibilities.**

This is a very simple example of surprise. Surprise is shorthand for anything that wakes up students and alerts them to the interest of your subject, anything that is out of the ordinary or makes them think. Whenever I have taught a lesson without surprise, I have found it harder work to engage students.

You can surprise with a starter, but the surprise can be the core of a lesson, or something repeated throughout a lesson—whatever it is, it should be something that makes the lesson memorable. You are looking for that 'what happened?' moment. In other words, if your students are ever asked 'what happened at school today?' ideally their answer will not only be that the head's trousers fell down, or that the geography teacher burst into tears. Your surprise should be one of the things they think of that brightened their day or made it interesting. One of the finest teachers I know taught most of an A-level maths class in the imaginary language of Venusian and got an 'outstanding' grading from his bewildered observer. It's all about style.

Every day is a five-lesson day

Surprise is necessary because boredom is a major problem in schools. As teachers, we can feel affronted when students say they are bored, and we often pretend that our colleagues never produce lacklustre lessons, 'holding the line' that education is never dull. Yet try tracking a student around school for a day, and you will remember how unrelenting school can be; how easy it is to tune out for a second and completely miss the task-setting; how at the end of a long day you simply don't care any more about what your teacher is so earnestly trying to tell you. As my son once put it when I complained about having to teach a five-lesson day: 'Hey, *every* day for me is a five-lesson day'.

A student saying 'this is boring' or 'I'm bored' is knowingly making a direct appeal to their teachers. It's a cry for help; don't fail to listen. Introducing surprise into your lessons is a way of signalling to them that for this lesson, at least, they will not be bored. Irritated perhaps. Challenged, hopefully. But not bored.

Learning by surprise

The way the school day is constituted breeds its own kind of monotony. As a teacher, you only have to think back to the last INSET day you went to, or the last conference you attended, to remember how hard it can be to concentrate all day without regular breaks, without time to absorb what you have just learned or practise it. In many schools, the push towards uniformity in teaching and learning leads to a school day that is increasingly devoid of variation, where students no longer delight in the prospect of having odd Mr Einstein for science, or eccentric Ms Shakespeare for English because they have long since been processed out of the system. Through the very nature of their academic expertise, most teachers are skilled in learning in a conventional style. I think of the young language teacher I worked with who confided in me that her Head of Department had unexpectedly walked into her lesson 'and they were all talking!' *Quelle horreur!*

It is easy to forget that the tradition of quiet study is not necessarily the best model for learning or for discovery; that Watson's final breakthrough about the double helical structure of DNA, for instance, reportedly came about not at a desk, but following what sounds like an alarmingly Freudian dream about two snakes intertwining. We are creatures of the world, and the world is our best teacher. Of *course* watching an apple fall to the ground is going to make you think harder about the nature of gravity than staring at a page in a textbook; of *course* seeing the crown jewels is going to make you understand more about the nature of being a king than the best PowerPoint display in the world. Real life is what interests students; real life is what they yearn towards when trapped in the classroom, and real life is what we should give them if we want them to stay interested in what we have to teach.

Surprise strategies

Use everyday objects

Try using commonplace things as a starter for your lesson. Anything that comes from the mysterious world outside school is a surprise once you are in lesson routine. Quite dull everyday bits and pieces become fascinating when placed in a school context. I have seen a group of students riveted by a set of keys, when they all had their own keys in their pockets; spellbound by a pile of old coins; fascinated by scraps of newspapers.

The beauty of using ordinary things as a surprise is that it does not need a huge amount of planning—just a little creativity. Placing a set of keys on the table and asking students how they relate to Macbeth, or to the structure of DNA, or to the accession of Queen Elizabeth I for instance, can elicit responses that you did not expect, as well as those you did. The point is that such objects make a connection between the 'real world' outside school and the world that you are trying to make them think about—and all too often they can forget those connections. Using a CD as an example of a circle, introducing a magnifying glass as a way of examining a source—such little things from the world outside school are the things that fascinate students. I've seen a set of left-handed scissors used as a stimulus for discussion that got a previously silent class debating equal rights for a whole lesson.

Critical thinking

Critical thinking, because it seeks to move outside the 'black box' of the classroom, is the friend of teachers wishing to surprise their students. The principles of critical thinking suggest that questions should be truly open in that the person asking the question should not have in their mind an answer that they are expecting the students to give.

GET WEAVING

Use a 'suggestion box' to gather questions from students that they really want to have debated.

Often in the classroom it is possible to observe a painful game of 'read my mind', where students are clearly used to a 'question—answer—validation' model. In this scenario, the teacher asks the question, the student answers, and the teacher confirms the correct answer with some approving words. Where this goes wrong is when the teacher asks a question expecting a certain answer, or certain type of answer, and the students do not respond as expected. Instead of investigating their responses, as each student answers, the teacher looks slightly disappointed, or says something like 'that's very interesting, but . . .?' looking around hopefully for the one telepathic child in the class. Critical thinking encourages answers to questions that offer more questions, and actively encourages students to question the teacher, debate first premises, and ask for further evidence before coming to any conclusion. It is fair to say that some teachers find this deeply uncomfortable—often because they may themselves have been trained in a system that promotes the giving of simple, 'accurate' answers to all questioning. Critical thinking seeks to empower students by getting them to think about the processes of their learning. At its best, it opens out questions which lead to genuine debate.

Learning questions

Try starting the lesson with a question on the board for students to discuss. A good example from science is to offer a picture of green people with the question 'why are we not green?' This question might get replies from students ranging from 'because we have no chlorophyll', or 'because we have benefited from an asteroidal impact several million years ago', through to 'because we envy no one', to 'we are not putrefying'. The responses themselves generate debate and engagement in science no matter what the focus of the lesson—from the moment the students walk in and consider this topic, they have stopped thinking about their last lesson, and are engaging with the new idea, thinking of how it relates to their new lesson. It is a route into the discussion which is a key part of any effective lesson.

Odd one out

An excellent, and simple, start to critical thinking is to offer students an 'odd one out' task, where they have to decide which of several choices is the 'odd one out', and why. A straightforward example would be a slide showing three portraits. The point is that there is no single answer, but many possible ones.

For instance, for a slide with pictures of Queen Elizabeth I, Shakespeare and Oscar Wilde, possible answers can be:

1. Queen Elizabeth, because she is a woman
2. William Shakespeare, because he is the only one with a beard
3. Oscar Wilde, because he is photographed, not painted
4. Shakespeare, because the other two have hats
5. Elizabeth, because the other two were poets and wrote plays
6. Shakespeare, because both the others were imprisoned
7. Wilde, because he was Irish

. . . and so on and so forth. The longer the game runs, the more you find out about what your students already know, and the more knowledge they share. Introducing further facts about the people concerned can then come to seem like simply an aid to the game, and so is taken enthusiastically, rather than seen as an imposition. You can start the lesson with the slide, when students may have relatively few ideas; then by the end of the lesson you can test them again and see how much longer they can keep up the discussion—visible progress!

Almost the same odd one out

Odd one out picture starters can consist of pictures of very similar things, and Google images is a wonderful tool for quickly generating this kind of starter—for instance for RE four pictures of staircases leading up to heaven (accompanied of course by the music 'Stairway to Heaven') with the question 'which is the odd one out and why?' allows us to discuss not just images of the afterlife, but how the details of images imply certain things about the nature of belief. Is a stairway curved, or straight? Wide, or narrow? With a railing or banister, or unprotected? What does it seem to be made of? Why are there flowers on one image? All these details can be examined fruitfully, and the process will help to teach students about how to read an image more carefully. In the same way, pictures of four people praying in different contexts and/or from different faith traditions will allow students to focus on points of similarity as well as difference.

Looking at images in this way can often 'slow down' students who are used to quick-fire imagery that constantly changes. It is a good way of improving attention span, demonstrating how much there is to be seen in a single slide. In the same way, the adolescent fascination with 'Where's Wally?' can be employed to draw in students to a challenging image. Getting them to pick out the difference between two almost identical pictures, or locate a specific list of items within a larger picture, both encourages students to look closely at detail and remember it.

Memory tables

A memory table is a small table at the front of the class with a range of items on it—these objects are connected to the theme of the lesson, and the students have to try and work out what this might be. It is a great way to focus students on a new topic, or to make them rethink aspects of a topic, as in the examples below:

History

To consider the ways in which Victorian women were different from women in the present day, a selection of objects from a handbag, with the instruction: 'Which of these do you think a Victorian woman could have owned?' is enough to start off a lively debate and also establish what students already know about the period.

Biology

To consider the features of evergreen and non-evergreen trees, have a number of different kinds of leaf on the table with the instruction: 'Which do you think comes from an evergreen plant'? This works especially well if you can include unusual leaves e.g. from succulents, and quickly establishes prior knowledge.

Maths

Have a set of everyday objects (seashells work well) displaying different kinds of symmetry with the initial task to decide which are symmetrical and in what way. You could then develop this into a discussion of radial symmetry, for instance.

Art

Assemble a number of objects which have been used for still life drawings by a variety of artists, and ask students to decide which objects they think would have been chosen by each artist. This is good for making them think about form and composition and similarities and differences between different artists.

Design technology

Place on the table a range of tools and a selection of made objects for which one of the tools would be necessary (e.g. a jigsaw), and ask students to guess which is the key tool for all the objects.

GET WEAVING

Taking one of the objects on a memory table away surreptitiously, and then asking students which one is missing, is a good way to encourage their focus on this kind of task.

Unusual objects and props

Even everyday objects can make lessons more interesting, but bringing in unusual artefacts can make a huge difference. Just as going to a museum where you can touch objects is immensely engaging for students, so bringing in unexpected artefacts is an excellent way of livening up the class. In RE, bringing in a realistic copy of a denarius is one vivid way to get students to think about the notion of payment and reward in the parable of the vineyard. I used to bring in a 'dragon fossil' for year 8 when working on scientific writing, which got them to consider the nature of scientific description remarkably rapidly. They also loved informing me why it had to be a fake.

To get students thinking mathematically, asking them to bring in objects that are in a certain mathematical shape can be really interesting. A display including Doritos, Toblerone packages and a cake slice as examples of triangles, for instance, can make connections to everyday life that will get students looking out for shapes everywhere they go.

Objects also stimulate critical thinking—because objects don't have right answers. In history, or science, or psychology try asking: 'What would a Victorian woman/ a medieval knight/ an ancient Egyptian think of this object?' as a good way to work out what students already know about a topic.

The power of touch

Tactile objects that students can actually stroke often soothe fidgety students who find it hard to concentrate. When teaching *Of Mice and Men*, where one of the main characters, Lennie, has a fixation about stroking soft things, I bring in different materials, including velvet (I draw the line at a dead mouse, as in the book), and get students to discuss their textures, and what they find pleasant to touch. Linked to key quotations from the book, this means that they never forget Lennie's interest. As homework, getting them to bring in something that Lennie would enjoy touching is unusual and engaging—and can make a terrific display.

Even subjects where students are used to touching things—such as PE or science—can be livened up by an intense focus on one aspect of touch. In physics, for instance, you can get students to close their eyes before touching different surfaces, then evaluate what those surfaces would be most useful for, or which surface would generate least friction. This gets them focusing immediately on texture in ways that otherwise would take a long time to develop.

Teaching with herbs

Linking everyday objects to a specific task can also be an opportunity to extend cross-curricular work. For this example, generally done as a revision lesson for year 11 English (because the time of year is just right for many herbs), you bring a selection of herbs into the lesson. A range which includes some pairs which look fairly similar, such as lemon balm and mint, lavender and rosemary, flat-leaf parsley and coriander works best, and creates a keener sense of competition, but any selection will do as long as it includes sufficient variety (do store them in separate bags, or the scents will mingle confusingly).

- Put a group of herbs on each table—generally this causes huge excitement, mainly from students who want to touch/smell/eat them, and they become more thrilled still when you permit them to touch and smell the plants.

- As they do so, you can start to inform them about the plants. You can do this with the help of scientific descriptions and pictures, or simply ask if students recognise any of the herbs, and talk through those which they don't know already, until each group is secure about each herb.

- Each person in the group then has to choose one of these plants, and write a paragraph of description about it that will identify it to the other groups. They are not allowed to use certain key words (depending on the herbs concerned) to make this more challenging.

- Immediately, this task focuses them on the details of description, and they quickly realise that if they can't use 'minty' or 'mint' to describe mint, they are going to have to become a little more inventive. After a while, they start to look closely at details of texture and structure, using connotations and similes and metaphors to make their description the most appealing.

It makes sense to link with as many other subjects as possible to enhance students' writing skills. This herb lesson makes a good link to scientific writing, and also brings in interesting possibilities for discussing the uses of herbs in different cultures for different purposes, or in the history of medicine (some herbs found in a medieval herb garden, such as Herb Robert, or Selfheal, are now regarded as weeds). It works well and produces effective written work, and it is a cheering lesson to teach on a stuffy afternoon when you would rather be out in the fresh air.

Sort cards

Sort cards are exceptionally useful when it comes to making students think differently, and in avoiding the negative teacher/student dynamic that encourages students to guess the right answer by reading your mind. If in doubt, I will turn a resource into a sorting exercise, because it has several virtues:

✓ Firstly, it encourages students to read what is on the cards—coloured cards, for some reason, are always read, when a piece of A4 paper with the same information on it would not be.

✓ Secondly, it gets students talking—even if all they are discussing is why on earth you have given them this task, they will actually be engaging with the information and with each other and with the problem.

✓ Thirdly, they will be forced to think about their own opinions—because there is no obviously right answer, they are freed up to argue their own ideas with their peers.

This kind of task is also especially good for students who have literacy problems, as it allows them to read only one slip of paper as part of a group, and to be informed by the reading of others, hence participating without pressure.

Once you have done sorting exercises a few times, students will get the hang of this, and start to work more quickly and efficiently at it. A good example in history, for instance, is to put a number of 'push' and 'pull' factors for a soldier deciding whether to join the army in WWI on a set of cards and ask students to decide which are most important—they internalise the main factors in order to have the debate, which gets you over the part where you have to inform them—they inform themselves so that they can participate in the task and the discussion. Similarly, in IT, you might put on cards the features of a website and get students to decide on the most important ones so as to allow them to internalise all the features required. A good example of a sorting exercise in design technology is to put the elements of a process on a set of sort cards to allow students to experiment with the most effective order and explain their choices—this helps them to internalise the reasons for that order. In maths, to ask students to sort a number of equations into increasing complexity can help to determine where students are in their understanding.

GET WEAVING

If you make sets of sort cards in different colours for different groups, this makes it immediately easy to sort them. You can cut up more than one set at a time if you do this, and also easily collect them into sets at the end of the lesson.

Matching cards

Using matching sort cards to focus students on terminology at the start of a lesson is a key cross-curricular literacy strategy. A set of sort cards with key vocabulary and definitions on them can be used to quickly embed new terminology. At the start of each lesson, students in groups match the definitions with their key words, helped by a display on the wall. As time goes on, you can gradually remove more key words from the display, as you cover their meaning in class, until all the students are confident about a large number of terms—you will find that they will also have learned how to spell them and recognise their spelling. Even in surprise, routine is of vital importance.

When using key words and definitions for sorting, try asking students which they think they will need for the forthcoming lesson, having shown them the lesson objectives. Another effective way of focusing on key words is to give students the definitions and ask them to write out the key word cards themselves, thus also giving them practice in spelling the terms correctly. Getting students to create their own key word word-webs also helps them to remember how to spell words through etymology or connections, and cards facilitate this way of working.

Music

Music is an immensely powerful tool in teaching, and one that is not used as much as it could be, especially given the ways in which it is now possible to use YouTube to quickly locate performances. Think for a moment of how it brightens you up to hear a favourite piece of music, makes you feel Christmassy to hear a carol, or soothes you to hear a classical piece and you will realise what a powerful tool we leave unused. Because music has such an influential force as an emotional trigger, you can get your students to associate new music that you play them with particular topics. Examples might include:

History
Triggers of time can be tied to genre. Nothing really creates a medieval feel as powerfully as playing some medieval music, and this is something that it is unlikely that students will have encountered in other subjects that day.

Music
Ask students to discover musical connections: What was the music of Hitler's youth? Why did Wagner affect him so powerfully? What about Rachmaninov makes you realise that this music was composed under the tsars?

English
Music is an especially powerful way of making cultural connections. Try, for instance, considering with what music the farm workers in *Of Mice and Men* might have been familiar. What was playing in Curley's wife's head when she thought about being a film star?

Geography
Try using music associated with a particular country when working on that country—or as a starter, to get students to guess a new topic.

Modern foreign languages (MFL)
You can use the same device—understanding the music of a country and the difference in sound is a start towards exploring a different culture.

Computing
Examining appropriate music to match with different features of a webpage, to enhance the message of each page, is an interesting extension activity.

Art and design

Using music to accompany an image will get students focused more quickly on a topic, and give cues to students who are less confident in making judgements.

PSHE

A variety of songs can be helpful to use as prompts for discussion. Madonna's coverage of female experience in 'Papa don't Preach' and 'Like a Virgin' can stimulate students to talk about female stereotypes and expectations, and some modern rap artists offer similar routes into a discussion of male stereotypes (though the theme music for *Top Gear* might give you an easy equivalent).

Citizenship

Robin Thicke's 'Blurred Lines' similarly starts off a ready-made debate about gender relations.

Media studies and film studies

Music should be something used in almost every lesson, so powerful is its ability to signal the introduction of a particular genre or a particular film.

Science

Music is also helpful—I've known teachers who use the music from the start of *Life on Earth* to give their students a sense of suitable grandeur in presentations, others who use the theme music from *The Big Bang Theory* to get their classes thinking, and for Astronomy, there is always Holst's *The Planets* or the music from *2001 A Space Odyssey*.

Maths

Of course there's the music from *Countdown* to add a sense of pace to quick arithmetical tasks and always the joys of Tom Lehrer's *'That's Mathematics'* song.

Politics

Discussing the use of music in film representations of current events is also powerful for learning—for instance, why the 'Ride of the Valkyries' is used in *Apocalypse Now*—linking back to Hitler, and the disjunction between genocide and beautiful music.

Behaviour management

The uses of music are many and varied. One of the simplest ways of getting a rowdy class quiet is to play music as the students come in, turn it up to stop them talking, then abruptly turn it down. In the sudden silence, you can start off with your first ideas.

Punctuality

This can be enhanced by music. When I taught one year 12 group Arthur Miller's *All My Sons* I had trouble getting them in class on time, as we were often in different rooms. I started playing Glen Miller's 'In the Mood' when I arrived in the room (appropriate for the period and helped them to remember the name of the author), and before long had the class trained to get there before the tune had finished. So powerful was this, that once when I was prevented by a faulty computer from playing the song, they were indignantly humming it as they came in.

This potent tool of music incidentally works as well on teachers as on students, and I have found it very helpful to play the class 'theme tune' in reframing my thoughts as I approach a different group and topic. Not to mention energising me at the end of a long day.

Images

I've already mentioned the value of pictures for starter activities, but images of all kinds are deeply powerful as a means of engaging students. Students who have lower levels of literacy will particularly relish the opportunity to 'read' an image in detail. To start a lesson by using a slide with a familiar object seen from an unusual angle gets students discussing possibilities, and fixed on your subject immediately. This works particularly well in science, where microscopic close-ups can become painterly and beautiful and baffling, though I have seen a microscopic image of a flea used to get students thinking about a John Donne poem; and a close-up of the bubonic plague bacterium is an interesting starter image for key stage 3 history. Images abound on the internet, and there are even sites devoted to the topic.

Humanities

You can play games such as 'Nazi Art Gallery' to discuss the arts and their connetion to political thought, putting up a selection of images around the room and asking students to evaluate which would have been considered acceptable to a particular culture.

English

Pictures that connect to particular poems or stories will engage students with the stories; asking them to 'read' the pictures as a first step towards studying a text, or using pictures to explain a concept—cubism, for instance, is really helpful in explaining some aspects of modernist poetry.

Maths

Images are an intrinsic way into learning, and the 'familiar object from an unusual angle' trick can be used to stimulate debate about polyhedra found in nature (images of viruses are particularly pretty).

PE, dance, music and drama

Images of people performing a task are a way into discussing how to improve performance—for instance in PE, demonstrations of different tennis players with snapshots rather than videos, were used to start a discussion about 'what happened next' in terms of action and technique.

Food technology

Images of ingredients can be used as the starter for a *Masterchef*-style invention task, where students are asked to write about what they could do with a given selection.

Thinking like a scientist

This works well as a way of livening up teaching, and is especially helpful in getting students to think about the processes of learning. Observing other teachers can work in the same way; this is quicker, easier and cheaper.

How it works is that you pick another teacher, and another subject. It might be a scientist, sometimes it's an artist, or historian, geographer, mathematician. Ideally go out of your comfort zone. Once you have the idea of this subject in your mind, you have to ask how they would approach your topic. So, for instance an English teacher has familiar ways of looking at a text. Think about it from the point of view of a different discipline, and you see it differently. So, you might look at artistic representations of a poem, or get students to write out single words in beautiful calligraphy to analyse them, draw graphs to track emotions in a novel chapter or play scene, consider the murder of Hamlet's father forensically, draw maps of events, or consider the reliability of a source, as in history.

Asking how a different kind of expert would approach a problem can lead to lively debate and discussion in class—and it stops you getting stale. It will also allow students to be the expert, as it is often they who are most experienced in recent pedagogy of other subjects. You can open it up to them to discuss how a scientist would tackle this learning problem—what information they would want to have—and immediately things in the classroom are livened up as the subject is looked at from an unfamiliar angle.

'Off-piste' learning

The ability to bring in 'off-piste' knowledge to help students see how you make connections between their learning and the outside world is one of the most valuable qualities in a teacher. Students often delight in the kind of odd snippets of information that you can find, for instance, in *The Guinness Book of Records* or the *QI Book of General Ignorance*. The 'Old QI' website http://old.qi.com/ has plenty of links to resources including a web forum where you can generate questions and get them answered by enthusiasts. A QI-style question to start a session is an excellent way of getting students to think about how their knowledge of a topic might be questioned in any subject.

Cross-curricular chats

These can be really helpful when you are trying to help students feel that you are not simply teaching to the test, but trying to help them learn something interesting that relates to their life outside and beyond school. If your subject makes connections with another, this can reinforce learning in both—you can even generate some cross-faculty work by teaming up and swapping teachers for sections of lessons.

I've seen some very good practice involving the teachers going into lessons and observing students talking about a topic so as to evaluate them for speaking and listening—there's no better way to get a shy student talking fluently than to put yourself into a context where you are clearly no longer the teacher-expert, and allow them to teach you about a topic. You could go into a maths lesson, and ask students to explain to you the concept they learned in that lesson, ask students in science to explain experimental method, pretend to drama students that you have to make a speech and ask for advice. In PE, try asking someone watching a football match to explain to you the off-side rule, or a refereeing decision, and you will find that there is often a fluent speaker hiding behind a normally quiet façade.

This sort of questioning can be an excellent way to get students thinking of themselves as fluent speakers—and is also an excellent behaviour management tool. If you find a particular student challenging, talking to him in a situation where you are not only not teaching him, but actually less knowledgeable than him, can redress the power balance in a way which will allow for more productive interactions.

Subject knowledge

Behaviour management is generally the aspect of teaching that trainee teachers ask about when they are anticipating their needs. Charlie Taylor is just one of many who suggests: 'The greatest fear trainee teachers have is that they won't be able to manage behaviour. It also remains one of the main reasons why teachers leave the profession.' But although behaviour management is important, a focus on it can lead to lessons where the main objective seems to be to keep the children in order—not to teach them. Remember that you are more than just a babysitter, and act accordingly.

GET WEAVING

Use the internet to upgrade your subject knowledge by listening in to videoed university lectures and public talks. There is even a specific University Lectures YouTube channel that you can browse for this.

What makes the key difference with behaviour is an effective and confident teacher—someone who has routines and plans, someone who knows their subject and enjoys it. Take the time to read around your subject—articles, books, journals—and share information that is new or cutting edge—particularly if it has nothing to do with examinations. Create a learning culture within your department—and if you are in a small department, make sure that you keep in touch with other teachers through professional organisations, or on the internet, so as to keep your professional curiosity alive. Try bringing in a critical article on a topic you teach, or asking students how they think you could make an idea appeal to students in a younger year group. Share and discuss critical ideas with students to model their learning. Avoid the impression that you are 'teaching to the test'; integrate what they learn in your lessons with the rest of their studies, and with the world outside.

If you are worried about how to translate your subject knowledge into student-friendly terms, good models of how to draw students into different subjects are readily available. The *Horrible Histories* series gives an excellent example of how to liven up for the younger key stages. The series of *New Scientist* books (based on their 'last word' column) that includes *Why don't Penguin's Feet Freeze?* and *Does Anything Eat Wasps?* is another format worth copying for science, while *The Music of the Primes* gives examples and ideas of how to make mathematics appeal, and John Sutherland's series of books including *Was Heathcliff a Murderer?* introduces literary puzzles. It's easy to move on from this kind of format to more sophisticated critical questions and responses such as the famous 'How Many Children had Lady Macbeth'?

These are only some of the ways in which teachers can surprise their students, and you will quickly find your own path. Whatever you choose to use, thinking of the lesson from the point of view of the students is a starting point. Imagine what would give you delight or interest you if someone were trying to teach you something you know nothing about and you won't go far wrong. You could come up with something far more inventive than anything I've suggested. Like teaching in Venusian.

Still wondering about the first question?

Well, you could say that the train driver minds the train and the teacher trains the mind—but I prefer the version which says: *Teachers tell you to spit out your gum, while the train driver says. . .*

Wait for it. . .

'Chew Chew!'

2

Purpose:
Making Maps

To forget one's purpose is the commonest form of stupidity.
(Friedrich Nietzsche)

> A mother mouse and a baby mouse are strolling down the street
> when a cat suddenly attacks them. The mother mouse says
> 'WOOF!' and the cat runs away.
>
> 'See?' says the mother mouse, '*Now* do you see why it's important
> to learn a foreign language?'

It is easy for teachers to forget the most important element of an
outstanding lesson; why you are doing it in the first place. Paradoxically,
it is particularly easy to forget this if you have planned your lesson well
because *you* know where you are going. For students, though, each lesson
is something new (hopefully), a point on their road of learning if you like,
and so lessons for them can be confusing if they are not clearly signposted.

Making purpose clear in a lesson

Some students—indeed, some parents—clearly think that teachers rock up each morning with no idea of what they are planning to do that day, and more or less make lessons up on the hoof. It might have been like that once (and the *Dead Poets' Society* fans wish it still was) but in these harsh OFSTED days there are few teachers who don't plan or follow schemes of work. It can be especially frustrating when students say, for instance 'I am going to the doctor/dentist/for my illicit family holiday next week and will not be in your lesson—will I miss anything?' My temptation is always to answer 'No, nothing at all— actually I'm just here to amuse everyone until it's time for your parents to come back from work, so one day is much the same as another. . .', but clearly this is not helpful. Sharing your purpose effectively with students at the start of a module and at the start of a lesson means that they will never again ask you what they'll miss. And for this alone it would be worthwhile.

But it's worthwhile in a wholly different way. Watching other people's lessons, particularly in a subject outside your own area, can act as a useful reminder of how important it is to signpost in each lesson as well. If you, as a non-expert, can't see where the lesson is heading, then the students probably can't either, and are likely to baulk, and become confused. Helping students to understand not only the purpose of a lesson, but how it fits into the whole scheme of things, means that they will understand the point of what you are doing, and be on your side with what you are trying to achieve. It's worth remembering that when you are observed, whether for OFSTED or performance management (or just from some friendly and keen person) your observer might well not be a subject specialist, and will likewise need those signals. Quite rightly, they won't think your lesson is outstanding if they have no idea what the point of it is.

Highlighting purpose

Given that you have (*please* tell me that you have) a clear idea of each scheme of work, with a long-term plan, medium-term plan, and if not a lesson by lesson plan, then at least a clear idea of how each lesson fits into that overall scheme, there is no reason not to share this information with students and parents. The clearer it is for them, the easier it will be for them to see why you are planning each lesson as you do. In university study, lecturers routinely share term plans and schemes for modules with the students—it is considered best practice so that they can become more independent, and work out which elements of the scheme fit into their final exams. There is no reason why we should not do the same for school students.

Creating an outline for parents and students

At the start of each school year, it is really helpful to give students an outline of the course, which explains what they will be doing each term, and what the point of this is. Students need to know the topics and skills that will be covered, the order in which they will be covered, how these relate to what they studied last year, and how they will relate to what they will study next year.

Once you have in place the basic structure of terms and modules, add in assessment times. This does not have to include precise dates (though it is great if you know when mocks or internal exams are and can put those in), but should at least include an assigned assessment week for the end of the module. Basically, students know at the start of the course that they will be doing some sort of assessment at this time, and parents can then try and avoid absence during that period.

This exercise can be immensely useful not only to students and parents, but also to staff, particularly new staff in a department. To have a clear sense of what is going on in a subject for any given year-group at any time creates a sense of shared purpose, which is essential when working effectively as a group of teachers. It also makes it easier to pool resources and share ideas.

Mapmaking

You can present your plans for the year, term, or module as a simple list, or a copy of the unit guide from an exam board, but if you have the time it makes more impact if you present it more creatively. Try formatting it as a table, a flow chart with arrows, or even as a literal map, as one creative colleague did, showing GCSEs as the final goal of a pilgrim's-progress-style venture. This last idea takes a little more time, but appeals to me more and more, with the potential that it offers for creating the Slough of Despond, or Giant Despair, as points to enliven students' perception of the journey towards their goal.

Whichever model you choose, stick it up, enlarged, on your classroom wall, and get students to stick a smaller copy into the front of their books so that they can refer to it, and check off lesson by lesson what they have done. If you do this, you can also take the books of students who are not present for any reason, and highlight the areas which they have missed in their 'maps', thus making it clear to them what they will need to do in order to catch up. Often you may find it more convenient to subdivide your maps, and here the image works well for students reared on Google maps, who will more readily understand how you want to 'zoom in' on a particular aspect of the curriculum for a time.

GET WEAVING

Use a pre-printed year planner and map out your year for the classes you teach using stickers or different colours for each class so that they can immediately see where key assessment dates are.

Publicity

Departments who advertise what they are doing tend to find students more focused and more ready to co-operate. It is worth having a curriculum map up on a display board outside class, for those corridor moments—I have even seen good joint displays where departments such as English and history have got together to create a timeline showing how their texts and topics interrelate with each other.

In departments where topics are taught all at the same time, it can help to have a display that changes week by week, so as to announce to those entering the department: 'This week in year 9 we are studying. . .Coastal erosion' (for instance). To this display you can then add on examples of good work, post-its from plenaries, and other elements that will make it appear up-to-the-minute.

Goals, learning objectives, and success criteria

Clear planning translates into clear learning objectives. Most schools and most teachers now use learning objectives for every lesson—indeed it can be rather depressing to see students, with Pavlovian enthusiasm, heading up their books with the 'LO' without any clear sense of how it might relate to their actual learning—but you need to be careful to make sure that your objective ties in closely with what you actually want to teach, and that you have distinguished between your goal, your learning objective, and your success criteria.

A goal is something that describes in fairly broad terms what your student will learn. Goals are rarely used for individual lessons, but might be useful for modules or units. An example of a goal would be: 'Students will gain an understanding of the role of the Great Depression in American history' or 'Students will appreciate a number of different religious traditions'. Goals tend to be characterised by verbs such as 'understand', 'appreciate', or 'know', and they will typically cover a wide area. A very common error when writing learning objectives is that they look more like goals—hard to measure, and hard to cover over a single lesson.

If, for instance, you want me to learn all about comets (your goal), then in a given lesson you might have a learning objective that means that by the end of the lesson I will understand one aspect of comets. But to say that my objective is to 'understand' is far too vague. How can you gauge that understanding? My success criteria might be that by the end of the lesson I should be able to describe how a comet is formed, or perhaps be able to name five famous comets, or even distinguish between a comet and an asteroid. Thinking in this way will allow you to not only formulate effective learning objectives and success criteria, but to differentiate effectively as well, with graduated learning objectives for different groups.

The Primary-school mnemonics 'WALT' (We Are Learning To) and 'WILF' (What I'm Looking For) can be useful here in helping you to distinguish between learning objectives (WALT) and Success criteria (WILF).

How to write a clear learning objective

Learning objectives should make clear the skill that will be gained by the end of the lesson. You need to ensure that your objective is skills-based rather than task-based. In other words, you do not want to describe the process that the students will go through, but what the students will be able to do when they have finished the lesson that they could not do before. Even for a knowledge-based objective this will be true.

The language of learning objectives is particularly important. Ideally, each objective should have three parts; a measureable verb, a condition under which the performance occurs, and the criterion of acceptable performance. For instance: 'Students will be able to identify three types of chord and their intervals without using their books.' Make sure that you avoid vague terms such as 'know' or 'understand' in favour of active verbs such as 'identify', 'explain', 'outline', and so on.

One good way of focusing your learning objectives is to use active verbs that reflect areas of Bloom's taxonomy. So, for instance, instead of 'look', 'think' and so on, use precise terms such as 'compare', or 'predict'. Active verbs alone are not enough. Often it is helpful to make the learning objective a two-stage process, with a first stage which will involve a lower-end activity such as naming or identifying an element and a second stage which encourages students to evaluate or compare. For examples, see Table 1 and compare the vague objectives on the left with the more precise ones on the right.

Using Bloom's taxonomy for writing learning objectives

Bloom's taxonomy has been around for a long time, as a way of thinking about stages of learning development, but is still useful when it comes to considering how to write learning objectives. In general, you want to be moving students up from the lower levels of Bloom's, where they are simply learning facts and figures, up through the application of that knowledge, to the final stage where they can analyse, compare and evaluate. For most subjects, these higher levels of Bloom's equate to the higher mark bands, and therefore to higher grades at GCSE and A-level.

Table 1 The difference between vague and precise learning objectives.

Vague learning objective	Precise learning objective
Appreciate the risks of developments in science and technology.	To distinguish between examples of perceived and actual risk arising from the application of scientific or technological developments.
Know the factors which have resulted in coastal erosion in Budmouth Bay.	To evaluate the three most significant factors of coastal erosion in Budmouth Bay.
Understand the elements of a healthy diet.	To decide six modifications of diet that would improve the health of a given client.
Know key terms for analysing poetry.	To be able to identify key poetic strategies in six poems.
Look at two paintings by Picasso and describe the differences between them.	To be able to compare painting techniques used in two paintings by Picasso.
Understand how plants grow.	To construct an experiment to determine which factors are most important for plant health.
Understand that there was more than one cause for the Peasants' Revolt.	To identify the difference between long-term and short-term causes of the Peasants' Revolt.

When choosing verbs for learning objectives, try to make sure that you are aware of the area of Bloom's to which they refer, so that you can move students upwards. Of course, there is always overlap, but the list in Table 2 is useful for quick reference.

Defining success criteria

Once you have your learning objective, it is important to distinguish this from your success criteria (remember WALT and WILF). There is a danger that your learning objective and your success criteria can become circular so that you decide that the objective of a lesson is to teach children to write in paragraphs, and the success criteria will be that they can write in paragraphs. It's not really quite that simple. The success criteria for an activity should consist of the evidence that the students have achieved the learning objective—so, in this example, if you really did set the unambitious objective 'to be able to write in paragraphs', the success criteria might be to produce four clearly linked paragraphs that change because of time, place, topic, and speaker. This would then lead you to realise that you would have to plan in an activity that would teach the rules for changing paragraphs, a subject to write on, and so on and so forth.

Table 2 Precise verbs for learning objectives matched to Bloom's taxonomy.

Level 1: Knowledge	Collect, define, describe, identify, match, name, recall, recognise, state, specify.
Level 2: Comprehension	Classify, differentiate, distinguish, estimate, explain, group, order, paraphrase, select, summarise.
Level 3: Application	Apply, calculate, choose, construct, demonstrate, examine, illustrate, predict.
Level 4: Analysis	Analyse, categorise, classify, compare, contrast, detect, examine, illustrate.
Level 5: Synthesis	Adapt, compose, construct, create, design, formulate, hypothesise, imagine, invent, modify, plan.
Level 6: Evaluation	Appraise, argue, evaluate, conclude, decide, deduce, defend, discriminate, justify, prioritise, rank, recommend.

I find it helpful to ask my students about success criteria when I set up a learning objective. I will ask them: 'How would I know that you are able to do this?' and they can then respond with their understanding of what success would entail—which also gives me a chance to clear up any misconceptions. In the example above, for instance, I would be able to explain that correct paragraphing is more than just breaking up the text at regular intervals. Table 3 gives examples of success criteria that you might use for the learning objectives in the earlier Table 1.

Note how success criteria tend to be specific and measurable—even more so than learning objectives. Sharing these criteria with students really helps them to understand what you are asking them to learn, and how to get there—and it is a great help to your own planning as well. Often I have worked on my learning objective, devised the success criteria, and then realised that I have in effect planned the whole lesson.

Table 3 Success criteria consists of the evidence that shows students have achieved the learning objective.

Learning objective	Success criteria
To distinguish between examples of perceived and actual risk arising from the application of scientific or technological developments.	Students produce four examples of perceived and actual risk, with an explanation of the difference between them.
To evaluate the three most significant factors of coastal erosion in Budmouth Bay.	Students describe at least six features of coastal erosion, and from these select those which they consider most significant for Budmouth Bay.
To decide six modifications of diet that would improve the health of a given client.	Students are able to describe at least six factors of a healthy diet, and decide how to relate these to the situation of the given client.
To be able to identify key poetic strategies in six poems.	Students can select quotations from the given poems to illustrate each poetic term.
To be able to compare painting techniques used in two paintings by Picasso.	Students can identify at least five techniques used in the two paintings.
To construct an experiment to determine which factors are most important for plant health.	Students can identify the key factors needed to keep plants healthy, and include them in their experiment.
To identify the difference between long-term and short-term causes of the Peasants' Revolt.	Students can name a number of causes for the Peasants' Revolt, and distinguish which are short-term and which are long-term.

Using a learning continuum

Another useful method to clarify goals is to stress to students the learning continuum, as outlined by Jackie Beere, where the learning objective is clarified through a stage-by-stage process that can be used to highlight differentiation.

A learning continuum is based on your learning objective, but shows the stages through which you need to pass to get to that objective. The easiest way to clarify these, visually, is as a series on a line moving from left to right, as in Figure 1.

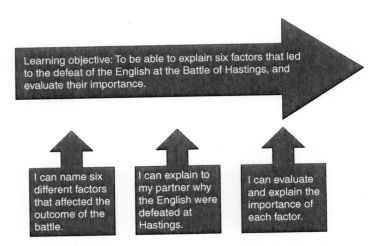

Figure 1 A learning continuum breaks down the stages of learning towards a final objective.

What a learning continuum does is break down the stages of learning towards the final objective, and in doing so allows you to pause through the lesson and evaluate how students are doing. I like to have a slide with the continuum on if I am using a PowerPoint, and then place it throughout the show, so as to allow students to use RAG (red-amber-green traffic light system) to rate the stages of learning. (If you have the time and energy, you can change the colour of the little boxes each time it comes up.) It also helps to make sure that you have a variety of learning activities so as to access each part of the continuum; for instance for the one above, I might first show students a video discussing the battle or get them to speculate on possible reasons for defeat in an 11th-century battle before we start. Knowing that I have to get them to a stage where they can discuss the battle with a partner helps me to plan the activity to generate that discussion.

Once you have set up a learning continuum, and get in the habit of thinking this way, it is much easier to share purpose with students, because they understand the processes of their own learning more clearly. I have found it especially good when helping NQTs and trainee teachers to plan, because it makes the lesson easier to chunk into manageable pieces, and avoids the tendency to let a starter activity carry on for too long.

'So that' targets

Linking your goals as a teacher to the students' goals is a productive way of letting the students see that you, like them, are working in a series of stages towards the final result. Making sure that your targets are linked to 'so that' phrases is another way of clearly connecting your purpose to task and result. With 'so that' phrases you clearly signal what the next stage of learning is and help to connect students to the final purpose of their work. You can do this within a lesson (e.g. 'we will learn to understand complex sentences *so that* we can write a paragraph showing a variety of sentence structures') or within a module (e.g. 'we will learn to plan and design three possible tables *so that* we will be able to choose one plan to build).

Keeping track with 'book buddies'

Part of sharing purpose means that you keep your students on track so that those who are absent or away realise that they have missed something. I have found that having 'book buddies' for students is one way to help deal with absentees, and deal with the problems created by students who come back into class uncertain of what they have missed. Book buddies are students who share responsibility for each other's work. They will often be seated together, and may already work together as peer markers. It helps if they are friends.

The responsibility of the book buddy is to make sure that their partner does not miss out if they are absent. If you are giving out handouts, hand out one for each absent student and get the book buddy to put the absentee's name on it so that when they return they will immediately have a copy of whatever they have missed.

Book buddies should be able to check that their partner's book records the progress of the course. They should also check that their books 'match' at the end of a lesson, and that they have filled in the stage that they have reached on their course map each session.

I have found book buddies invaluable for reminding me when their paired students have been away or missed homework. If you are not dealing with chronic absenteeism, then their responsibility is not usually very great, but it is very clear, which is helpful. As a plenary exercise, you can get students to write in each other's books what they have learned in a given lesson. If one student is away this can then be a really useful prompt for them when they return.

GET WEAVING

At the end of a lesson, encourage students to look through each other's books and compare work done for a given lesson. This helps to sharpen up presentation and completion rates for work.

Get students planning for you

This may sound callous (or lazy?) but getting students to plan out their own learning is one of the most effective things that you can do to help them have a clear sense of purpose. I learned about this when I was working with two particularly challenging groups. I was teaching them for a controlled assessment, but had covered all the content that we needed to do—the remaining lessons were simply preparing them to tackle the question. They were a little weary (as was I) of the topic, and kept asking me when we were going to have a 'fun' lesson—i.e. one in which they did not have to do any work. I felt that learning was starting to be something they felt was 'done' to them, and not something that they did. Finally, I decided on drastic action.

The students were told that they would be designing future lessons, which excited them no end, and then we had a lesson looking at the Controlled Assessment (CA) task. They were given some examples of good work, which they evaluated, and asked to decide what we needed to do in order to get their work up to that standard. Offered a selection of possible teaching methods and resources, they had to plan out what would best prepare them for the task in two weeks' time. Absolute freedom of choice was given, but they had to agree as a class on the plan, and come up with a list of at least ten things that they wanted to do in order to help them with their learning.

Of course one of these things was 'watch a video', but equally, given the parameters of the task, it could not be the only thing. Slowly, they started to think seriously about what they needed to do to get their work up to a reasonable standard. It was one of the most productive sessions that I have ever had, because for the first time they were starting to think about what I was up to—the teacher changed from being someone who just turned up on a daily basis to torment them into someone who was trying to help them. Students started remarking that they hadn't realised how much thought must be put into their lessons, and that they now understood that teaching must be pretty difficult.

The final plan from both groups contained pretty much all the activities that I would have planned for myself, with the great difference that the students were completely on board with it. In subsequent lessons, the plan was put on the wall, and we crossed off each activity as we did it so that they could see their own progress. They each had a copy of the plan, which they likewise ticked off as the lessons progressed. This is now a strategy that I use regularly to help students become more independent learners. It works well with all age groups, and across a range of subjects.

Purposeful starters

One easy way to establish shared goals is to make them a part of a starter activity. Using post-it notes at the start of a lesson to ask students to set a personal target can be invaluable in gauging the mood of your class that day, in finding the things that students themselves are worried about, and in focusing them upon their own role in their learning.

A favourite tactic of mine is to set out the learning objective, explain that this is what I would like the students to learn, and then ask them what *they* want to achieve in this lesson. You should make clear that this might be the learning objective, but that it could be something else, even something as simple as trying to ask a question. Written on a post-it, then put on their desks, or on a board, the target remains as a visible reminder of their own purpose: a concrete goal. Looking at these notes you can quickly see the mood of a class, and where they need more extension or more personal help. Sometimes students can also use this as a way of opening out their own wider feelings about school, such as: 'Today I want to stay in lessons, even if I don't look as though I do', or 'Today I want to be picked when I put my hand up'. This type of request is very easy to grant, and immediately engages students with the learning.

Following this up with another post-it task at the end of the lesson, where students have to write down what they achieved, can be equally revealing. If you use the formula: 'It can be the same thing that you planned, or it may be something completely different that surprised you', this opens out the possibility of students moving beyond their initial ambitions.

Most of the time, these responses are very positive, and heartening, but sometimes they can pose a real challenge. Occasionally, you might even see 'I learned nothing', and although this can be hard to face, it is an invaluable starting point for a conversation with that child about their previous knowledge, their difficulties with learning, or their overall response to your subject. I remember looking at one student's note, after he had been difficult and disruptive through the lesson, and seeing written 'I *did* try, but it was hard for me'. This not only engaged my sympathies, but also encouraged me to put in place some more radical differentiation for him, something that resulted in a much more productive working relationship.

Reminders

It's not enough, though it is important, to establish your purpose at the start of the lesson. Throughout a lesson you need to refer back to your purpose, having 'mini plenaries' to check progress and remind students of where they are heading. The learning continuum can be useful for this, but if you don't use one, then do still refer back to your learning objective throughout the lesson. One good way of doing this is to select some unfortunate student to remind you of it at regular intervals (not the same student every time, or you will drive them to a nervous breakdown). Ask students how the activity that they are doing connects to their learning objective—what is the purpose of what they are doing at that point? If what they are doing is staring out of the window, or poking their friend's eye out with a sharp pencil, then this will be a gentle reminder to stay on task.

Invisible sun

This is the strategy of *not* sharing your learning objective with the students. Instead, you have it on the board, covered up. Their task is to try and work out, by the end of the lesson, what the objective of the lesson is. This idea takes a really confident and cool-headed teacher to carry it off. I've seen it done, and it worked brilliantly—but I've also seen it attempted when it was a bit messy, and worked far less well, so use it with caution, and never as a substitute for planning.

This idea works especially well with the checking strategy, as students have to keep speculating about the purpose of their tasks, and if you are checking and reminding them that they have to find out the purpose, they will often be enthusiastic about solving the mystery; there's a real sense of achievement when they get it right. If you have given them a clear sense of purpose at the start of the module, and in the other lessons throughout, this can be a good way of waking them up and making sure they are alert to the wider purpose of their lessons.

Focus on skills

If you are teaching a lesson, and you know that certain students are not that enthused about doing it (this can often happen when subjects are compulsory, or even in the final year of an option subject), then do make sure that you clarify for students the connections that your subject has with other subjects that they may be more enthusiastic about. Reminding a keen footballer, for instance, that he really should practise his speaking skills, as he will no doubt be giving interviews one day, or explaining to students about to debate a topic that they may be having to argue their case at work, so they should practise extracting relevant data details now, can often add an extra energy to otherwise everyday tasks.

I have a colleague who used to be in the army, and who is regarded as an extremely cool teacher by students as a result. He has done us all the great favour of emphasising to students how important it is to be able to read and write fluently, pointing out to them the numerous occasions when he had to use these skills in the army, and how hard it was to have to quickly read and understand instructions and then relay them to his team. Because he's not an English teacher, his words of wisdom are taken that much more seriously, and he has had a noticeable impact on some students' attitudes to literacy.

Making this kind of connection to the world of work can really help—for instance, discussing when map-reading will come in handy, or when being able to judge a source, or evaluate an experiment will be helpful. Keeping in touch with the news is a good way of doing this, as you can often make connections between events in the public eye and particular subject areas. I know an art teacher who enthused her Key Stage 3 classes after a painting by a famous artist was discovered locally in someone's attic, by saying quietly 'well, of course *you'd* all be able to recognise a medieval painting if you saw it, wouldn't you. . .what would have been the key features again?'

GET WEAVING

To help students focus on skills for work, try setting a homework which asks them to audit the skills their parents have used in adult life that relate to your subject. If you create your audit carefully you should find that all parents have some relevant skills.

Aspirational learning

In the current climate of education, it is easy to get too exam-focused in learning, and this can squeeze all the joy out of school. When thinking of the purpose in lessons, it is important not to focus only on the purpose that relates to exams. If you remember the lessons that you enjoyed as a child, they are unlikely to be the exam-focused ones, and children nowadays are more examined and tested than perhaps they have been at any time in history. Instead, try and make connections wherever possible between what you are doing and life outside the school. Apart from anything else, this enhances children's cultural knowledge, and helps them to feel connected to the wider world.

I know that students enjoy it when I reference the outside world, and remark that a particular piece of knowledge might help them win *Countdown* or *Mastermind*, or a pub quiz one day. More than this, if you reference other classes, children enjoy it. I will often say to a year 7 class that I am going to try something on them that I would usually only teach to year 9, or tell year 10 that we are going to try some A-level work. It is a sure-fire way of getting them interested because they will be thinking of learning and knowledge as something interesting for its own sake, and not as something that they are doing for you.

Ultimately, making purpose clear is simply answering the question—so often asked, openly or silently by school students—'What is the point of all this?' Once you have answered this, and put the idea in their minds that there actually is a point to it, and a good one, then you can really start teaching them purposefully.

3

Investigation: Doing it for Themselves

We cannot teach people anything; we can only help them discover it.
(Galileo)

Can you put the following teaching methods in order of effectiveness?

Lecturing
Teaching others
Reading
Demonstration
Audio-visual
Group discussion
Practice

Much research has established that traditional teaching methods are not always the most effective. The image of a teacher standing at the front while students listen and take notes—so beloved by many not involved in everyday education—has been shown to be one of the least effective ways of ensuring that information is learned.

In fact the apocryphal 'learning pyramid' below, which supposedly rates different methods of communication against each other in terms of effectiveness (in this case, the retention of knowledge two weeks after teaching), is something of an educational urban myth. Hard research to back up its suspiciously neat statistics is difficult to find. But it is a useful reminder of how helpful it can be to avoid a single style of learning, and how helpful it can be to let students try things out for themselves. In the 'learning pyramid' model, lecturing someone means that they take in about 5% of what you say, whereas teaching someone else achieves a 95% retention rate. People have accepted these statistics without investigation because they seem to rehearse a self-evident truth. At one level, it seems obvious—to teach something you have to understand it yourself—but the reality is more complex than this model might suggest. To explain a concept to a class is, once you know it yourself, fairly straightforward—but to set things up so that they can discover it for themselves can take a lot more work.

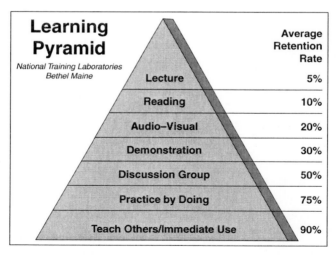

Learning Pyramid National Training Laboratories Bethel Maine	Average Retention Rate
Lecture	5%
Reading	10%
Audio–Visual	20%
Demonstration	30%
Discussion Group	50%
Practice by Doing	75%
Teach Others/Immediate Use	90%

Figure 2 The effectiveness of different levels of communication.

Investigation should always be a part of your lessons; it is not only effective as a teaching tool, it is invaluable as a behavioural one. Students who will fret if asked to stay still and listen will be far more manageable if they know that they can count on a time in your lessons when they will be able to discuss ideas with their peers. But it can be difficult to let go of the model that says that the ideal classroom is one where students are sitting silently writing or listening to the teacher. In order to allow your students to investigate, you may have to revitalise your own practice in terms of questioning and organisation. Don't worry; it will be worth it.

Ways to investigate

Set up effective group work

Setting up group work is more than just dividing students and letting them go—to work effectively it has to be meticulously planned. To make a group task work, you have to set up not only parameters for group discussion and behaviour, you also have to set up the task to ensure that it will be effective. Any group task should include the following:

a. **A clear reference to the learning objective** Students must be able to see how their group work will relate to the lesson as a whole.

b. **Clear task words** Avoid using vague terms such as 'discuss'—give them a problem to solve or an issue to evaluate or annotation to complete.

c. **Clarify the result** What will students be expected to do at the end of the group work (e.g. present back to the class) or what should they have produced (e.g. a marked script)? If you can offer a model of previous good group work that would be helpful in letting them know your expectations.

d. **Time limit** Make sure students know how long they have, and that this time is a realistic length for them to achieve all that they have to do. It can help if you keep reminding them of the time (by now you should have. . . you have 5 minutes left. . . you should be writing up) or you could use a timekeeper as one of the roles for the group.

e. Share the work Students must not work in isolation, so they need to get a sense of how the rest of the class has done at the task. Students can learn a great deal from seeing how their peers deal with group work, and what they produce.

f. Use the work Make sure that you show how the different groups have contributed to final conclusions, and that the learning is explicit. Build into your plenary comments about work from the groups. Always praise good work, and be clear and effective about what is praiseworthy—'blanket praise' is not helpful and students see right through it.

Create thought-out groups

Good group work comes from careful thinking about the composition of a group, and from knowing your students well. Don't, whatever you do, put Angry Sam into a group with Terrified Tina without realising what this entails, or you are setting them both up to fail. Think carefully about the kind of work you want them to do, and work to each student's strengths. The following are just some examples of how you can group students in class:

Ability

Traditional, and none the worse for that, ability grouping is one of the most popular forms of grouping used in schools. In this model, you put together all the students who are working at a particular level, so that each group is composed of students of a similar ability. The advantages are that you can easily provide differentiated resources at an appropriate level for a particular group, and focus support on those students who most need it by putting them in the same group. The disadvantages are that students can become complacent and unlikely to move from their allotted range. Don't think that differentiation will be easier with this kind of grouping—you should still differentiate and give opportunities for extension within each group, and of course those who need support may not all be at the same level.

Mixed ability

If done well, this works well, but all too often it ends up as a last-minute plan by a teacher who has decided that ability grouping isn't working. With mixed-ability grouping you make sure that each group contains a range of ability. You can either do this so that the students are working with cognate ranges—so for instance from level 5c to 4c in one group—or so that students reflect the range of abilities throughout the class. If you do the latter, you have only multiplied your original problems of differentiation, and you are also unlikely to be able to create a real range equally in all groups, so the former is probably the most practicable.

Behaviour

Another popular option—this kind of grouping distributes students in different groups by looking at their behaviour rather than their ability—put crudely, you try and split up the problem students, and make sure that you only have one in each group. The theory is that the good students in each group will tame the wild ones, and make the class work more productively. In practice it often means that the more challenging students will stir up the docile ones and infuriate them by not staying on task. I often find it is easier to put all the tricky students into one group, which I can then give additional support to. It also forces them to take some responsibility for the task themselves, which is a welcome novelty.

Friendship

Probably the least popular way of grouping for teachers, but worth considering, because students adore it. The reason why students are generally not allowed to work in friendship groups by teachers is because it is assumed that they will spend all their time chatting and be off-task. However, this means that working with your friends has become such a rarity that it is a real bribe. I have very successfully allowed students to choose friendship groups for work under three conditions:

1. No one in the class must be left out.

2. They have to decide on their groups within 30 seconds (timed).

3. If they do not work productively, the groups are changed and they are not allowed to complain.

Given these essential rules, friendship groups work well, and can be wonderfully supportive. I have found it particularly good at helping students who are finding it hard to integrate with the rest of the class— the first rule means that they are in demand, as the other students can see their chance of working with their friends vanishing if anyone is left out.

Jigsawing

I love jigsawing, because it does seem to increase the pace of a lesson and helps people not to feel left out. With this strategy, you will need cards that have on one side numbers and on the other side symbols. The numbers and symbols are coordinated so that for instance you have a star 1,2,3,4,5 and a circle 1,2,3,4,5. You will need to do a little basic maths to work out how many cards you need—a five by five set will deal with a group of 25, so you might need a few duplicates, depending on the group size you want.

You distribute the cards, and students get into groups by looking at the numbers, and then investigate the first task as a group, focusing on a particular aspect of that task (for instance, they might annotate a text concentrating only on the language used, or investigate a source from one perspective, or evaluate an experiment using a particular set of criteria).

Once the students have completed this first element of the task, you ask them to re-group, this time using the symbols so that you have a circle group, a triangle group and so on. In each new group you will then have a representative from each first group, whose responsibility is to explain what they have discovered to the rest of the group. Jigsawing is especially good for helping shyer students to participate, and for stirring up those who tend to allow others to do the work in group tasks.

Shepherd and sheep

This type of group work is good if you have a few leaders in your class who always want to take over. Basically, you fulfil their dream—but give them some serious responsibility. They are the shepherds, and they are responsible for getting their sheep (that is, the rest of the group) working well—by completing the task, and all participating. The sheep are responsible for objecting to the shepherd's plans, and coming up with reasons why they should do it differently, but also have a responsibility to complete the task. The winning group is the one which gets the task completed most effectively. Not a strategy to try if you are nervous about lively discussion, but paradoxically it stops students acting like sheep.

Really random

In this grouping strategy, you use a random name generator to sort out your groups for you. You can do the same thing by using part of a pack of cards, and dealing them out without planning. The remit for students is that they have to get on with the random group members that they are assigned, and as a reward will be able to choose their groups next time. This is really good for making students work more co-operatively and getting them to look beyond the immediacies of friendship groups. Often they find out something surprising about the groups formed. I have also found it invaluable for shaking up my own grouping strategies, and allowing combinations that I might not have risked left to myself.

Power play

This works well if you have some students who dislike group work because they always end up doing all the work. You can identify these 'primary leader' students either through a brief quiz or through observation, and then put them in a group by themselves, perhaps with a slightly more demanding or complex task. You may find that this results in some awkwardness from the other students who are used to being led and uncomfortable without them, but you will find that it will encourage 'secondary leaders' within that group, and also allow the primary leaders to enjoy being in a group without having to lead it. Often this group will need to develop new skills so as to ensure that they work effectively.

Give me five

In this group strategy, you need groups of five (it does work with six or seven, but the name isn't so good!). Each person in the group has to try out one of five methods of approaching a task. They then move to another group and have to try out a strategy they have not yet used. If, for instance, you are asking students to investigate a text, you allot tasks as follows:

1. Summarise it in 50 words.

2. Highlight five key points.

3. Think of five effective sub-headings.

4. Select the five most important words, and give reasons for your choice.

5. Draw five pictures to illustrate it.

Each of these tasks require students to approach and understand the text in a different way, and letting them try out all five strategies can mean they then become more prepared to explore new methods of learning.

Give students roles in groups

If you create roles in groups, you give each student a remit for their interaction within the group so that they have a clear task to complete. This means that (depending on the task) they are asked to be (for instance) leader, recorder, director, scribe, spokesperson, analyst, judge and so on. The advantage of this is that you can use the magic of the laminated card to assign roles, and that you can change the roles depending on your task. It also means that no student has an excuse to do nothing.

GET WEAVING

Ensure that students know that they will be doing group work the lesson before, or even tell them their groups so that they have a chance to think about their possible roles.

This type of group work does require a little thought and planning out before the lesson, but a good set of roles, once set up and established with a class, can be used and re-used profitably many times. For different tasks and different subjects you may find that you will create your own combination of role, but some useful sets of roles for different tasks which have proven useful across a range of subjects are as follows (please note that the names are only for convenience; you can perfectly well use scientific enquiry for drama):

Editorial team

- Project manager (in charge of ordering final outcome)
- Recorder (takes notes and prepares presentation)
- Checker (ensures data is accurate, and that data reinforces points)
- Spokesperson (presents outcomes to class)

Business meeting

- Chair (keeps order and ensures fair turn taking)
- Secretary (takes minutes)
- Observer (records an overview of the discussion)
- Timekeeper (ensures fair time is given to each argument)
- Spokesperson (for and against)

Political debate

- Proposer (offers a proposition)
- Opposer (opposes the proposition)
- Supporter (one for each side; can multi-role)
- Devil's advocate (tries to pick holes in discussion)
- Sceptic (objects with reasons)
- Summariser (sums up discussion for presentation)

Scientific enquiry

- Director/moderator (controls discussion)
- Data analyst (selects and tests data)
- Reflector (reflects back to individuals their understanding of what has been said for checking)
- Questioner (comes up with questions to solve)
- Illustrator (records discussion in written or diagrammatic form)

Hot off the press

- Facilitator (keeps order in discussion)
- Recorder (records what has been discussed)
- Reporter (reports back at the end of the session)
- Runner (acts as liaison between group and other groups or teacher)
- Elaborator (makes connections between discussion and wider world)

Playmaker

- Director (manages discussion and keeps focus on objective)
- Producer (responsible for drawing in wider elements to discussion)
- Technician (manages data details)
- Scriptwriter (writes out/records discussion details)
- Performer (presents final results to class)

Use (and teach) Bloom's taxonomy

Bloom's taxonomy can be a useful framework for working out questioning strategies that help students become more independent investigators. The six layers of questioning can be summarised thus:

a. Knowledge (recalling facts and figures)

b. Comprehension (checking understanding of information recalled)

c. Application (considering the practical relevance of information)

d. Analysis (investigating and selecting elements of the information)

e. Synthesis (using information to move forward in a creative way)

f. Evaluation (making judgements about information)

In general, lower-order questions will ask students to retrieve information, respond to simple queries, give a 'yes' or 'no' answer, stick to the point, retrieve facts and figures, and answer comprehension questions. The danger of these is that they can produce a response without any real understanding taking place. Badly phrased questions will allow students to guess the answer—and if it is phrased as a 'yes' or 'no' response they have a chance of getting it right anyway.

Higher-order questions will tend to ask students to interpret ideas, speculate about possibilities, consider different interpretations, evaluate views, give opinions, explain why something is important and imagine different ways of doing things. Understandably, these questions tend to be much more popular with students. I have found, interestingly, that higher-order questions are often more effective than lower order ones for testing basic knowledge of facts and figures, because they demand that students actually think about the significance of the answer in a wider sense.

Being Sherlock Holmes

It is useful when students themselves understand the difference between higher and lower-order questioning. To help students do this, I tend to refer to Sherlock Holmes and Dr Watson (bless the BBC for remaking the series for a new generation).

Dr Watson, of course, tends to ask the lower-order questions—who, what, where, when—and asks closed questions. Sherlock, by contrast, will tend to ask higher-order questions—why, how, which, explain—and will ask open questions which invite speculation. Nobody really wants to be Dr Watson.

Devise blooming circles

For some reason, students will often find answering lists of questions wearisome, and often leave them unfinished. Setting questions in circles works much more effectively, because it gives a sense of both choice and progression, while using Bloom's for questioning is an inbuilt system of differentiation, so combining these two strategies works especially well. If you set an image, a text or a problem in the centre of a landscape page, you can then set out a number of question boxes around it. I tend to use six, one for each level of Bloom's, though of course you can change this; for groups differentiated over a smaller range, you could have several questions at a similar level.

Once you have your boxes, you include questions in each, written at the appropriate level. Students may choose which order they answer the questions in, and select the ones that they find most interesting.

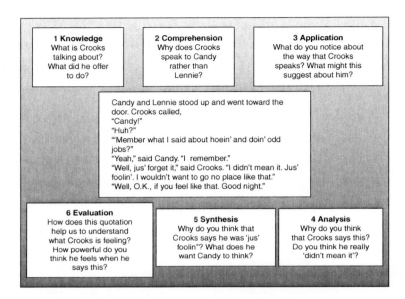

Figure 3 Questions in a circle around a central text, one for each level of Bloom's taxonomy.

Figure 3 shows an example for English, where students are being asked to comment on a small section of text.

Once you have accustomed students to working in this way, you can ask them to create their own 'blooming circles', at first giving them question prompts. Creating a question means, of course, creating or speculating on an answer, and just as with single best answer quizzes, you can encourage students to investigate issues or texts or sources or experiments and in the process help them to become more independent. Figure 4 is an example of such a circle with question prompts for the same novel, with students being asked to choose their own passage for comment as well as devise their own questions.

Students rapidly become accustomed to the idea of devising questions about texts, and with little encouragement will get into good habits of investigation. Figure 5 is an example from RE, where students were given a picture cue in the centre (of a man praying) and asked to devise a series of questions about it using Bloom's. These then formed the basis for discussion in the class afterwards. Figure 5 shows an example.

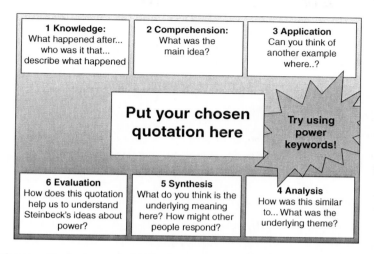

Figure 4 Students can devise their own question for a 'blooming circle'.

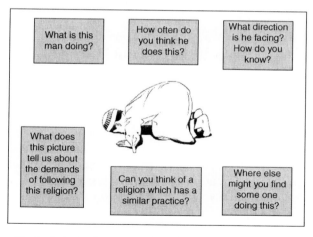

Figure 5 Student-devised questions based on Bloom's taxonomy, arising from the illustration.

Create tasks that aren't fluffy widgets

If you are in any doubt about the idea that traditional comprehension questions may exclude or limit the learning of your students, try the exercise below:

Fluffy widgets

In Mensurable season, widgets of the slmenty variety may become fluffy, and leave the colony to seek out sporking opportunities with other widgets. This opportunity can give them a drummal advantage over non-fluffy widgets, who are unable to spork as widely, and may therefore translate to better colony health.

However, those fluffy widgets who spork outside the colony have an additional risk. Frequent sporking reduces a widget's kiolade ratio, and this is of course a risk, as a widget with a low kiolade ratio is unable to pilloloy.

a. Which variety of widgets become fluffy?

b. When do widgets tend to become fluffy?

c. What are fluffy widgets especially likely to do?

d. Are there any problems associated with frequent sporking?

EXTENSION: What are the risks of an overly low kiolade ratio?

It is sometimes helpful to 'fluffy widget' a worksheet—in other words, if your questions can be transformed into a worksheet that is still answerable if you change all the key words into meaningless ones, then it is probably not teaching your students anything beyond basic information retrieval. Try considering how you could really test knowledge of widgets:

i. Draw the life-cycle of a widget.

ii. Describe the ideal habitat for a widget, and explain why it is suitable.

iii. Explain what animal the widget might be most closely related to and why.

Task-setting and questioning are very closely connected; any of these higher-order tasks will tend to engage students more keenly, and also test their knowledge much more sharply. Thinking of more demanding tasks will also make you re-evaluate how you supply information to students, and what information they will need to complete the task.

Use single best answer quizzes

These kinds of quiz are a much more effective type of questioning than traditional multiple choice, yet they will still allow for quick marking. They are now used by many universities for higher-level courses, but are still really useful for school students, because they demand that they think deeply about the issue being questioned. In a single best answer quiz, all the answers offered are potentially correct, or have some elements of truth to them, but only one answer is actually correct. Examples might be:

Quiz on chapter 1 of *Lord of the Flies*
What first suggests to the reader that Ralph does not really want to be friends with the fat boy?

a. Ralph does not ask him his name in return when he asks his, but moves away after the boy starts to talk to him.

b. Ralph leaves him behind so that he can get to the beach first.

c. When Golding says Ralph 'tripped over a branch and came down with a crash' this suggests that pride comes before a fall.

d. Golding uses the words 'disentangled' and 'stole away' to suggest that Ralph is sneaky about leaving the fat boy.

Quiz on coastal erosion
Which one of the following factors is MOST responsible for the day-to-day changes along a coastline?

a. changes in sea level

b. climate change

c. human activity

d. the work of waves

e. the nature of the shoreline

Quiz on cells

Which of the following is NOT true of a cell?

a. It is the basic structural unit of life.

b. Mitochondria are found in both plant and animal cells.

c. The cell membrane allows all substances to pass in and out of the cell.

d. All organisms are made of one or more cells.

e. The membrane-bound structures within most cells are called organelles.

You can get students to set single best answer quizzes on a topic for themselves, and then use these questions to test other students in a group, or another group. I once successfully had two parallel groups setting reading quizzes for each other over a whole term—they got more and more competitive, and the quizzes more and more complex as the term went on, with excellent results.

GET WEAVING

You can use single best answer quizzes to give students information as well as to test it. Answers can model for students the way to write or to think about different options.

Use investigation grids

An investigation grid is a four by four grid of boxes which you supply to students who are looking at something and trying to investigate. You ask the students to fill in each box in the grid with a question that they think it would be interesting to have answered. For weaker students you can start them off with a question or two, or model the questioning in the same way as you did for the Blooming circles.

The grid shape does seem to encourage students to come up with more questions than they would do with a blank sheet—the imperative to fill in those little boxes is a strong one. You can then use the grids as the basis for each group's investigation, or jigsaw students to let them see who has come up with the same or similar questions—this targets their discussion on something that they are genuinely interested in, rather than on your chosen focus, meaning that they are far more likely to come up with their own independent conclusions.

Investigation grids seem to work across all subjects, though different subject areas use them differently. In English, for instance, students might speculate about issues outside a text, or ask how a mobile phone would have affected the outcome of a novel, while in DT they might focus on how their design could relate to other designs.

The beauty of an investigation grid is the ways in which it fosters independent learning, so don't be afraid of what may seem to be 'random' questions. Being allowed to ask and answer what may seem to be irrelevant questions enthuses students, encourages them to research for themselves (you can always set the answering of these questions as a homework task) and gives them a precious sense of control over their learning.

Below is an example investigation grid for the water cycle:

How long does it take snow to melt?	Do clouds always form over seas?	If clouds are like steam, why aren't they hot?	If the earth was all at the same level, would we still have rivers?
Does the height of a mountain affect river flow?	How much water is trapped in clouds at any one time?	Why does rain not fall so much in deserts?	How does water get underground?
How warm does it have to be to evaporate water?	Does water always evaporate at the same speed?	What happens to the salt in seawater when it evaporates?	Could we turn the seas into fresh water?
Does it take a lot of energy to evaporate a litre of water?	What would happen if it didn't rain for a year?	Could we make artificial clouds?	Why don't clouds drop rain straight back into the sea?

Figure 6 Investigation grid for the water cycle.

Develop your own questioning skills

Teachers use between 400 and 500 questions a day, but the vast majority of these are lower-order questions, which are either instructional or informational. Lower-order questions are those which sit on the lower half of Bloom's taxonomy, so tend to test knowledge, comprehension or application. They have their place, but increasing higher-order questions to even 50% of the questions that you use is shown to have an improvement in student attainment and achievement, so it's well worth a try.

Having said that, it can be hard to get out of the habit of using lower-order questions. It reminds me of the parenting advice to say three positive things for every negative one that you say to a toddler—really difficult when you can be reduced to 'well done for *not* eating that mud' in a desperate attempt to counteract the number of times that you have chastised them for doing something potentially fatal. Teaching can sometimes feel a bit like that, so you may need to provide yourself with a 'script' for questioning to help yourself out.

Refreshing questioning

Use the grid in figure 7 (I print it out and put it on my teaching desk) as a reminder of the different things that you could do to help facilitate group discussion. If you have not tried any of these strategies recently, perhaps it is worthwhile giving them a go.

Avoid meaningless questions

Questions such as 'Do you understand?', 'OK?' and 'All right?' generally are interpreted by students as needing no response, or demanding only a positive one. In general, try to avoid these, as they are just nervous tics, and project insecurity on your part. Turning them into statements makes them much more powerful and means that they can become real checks: 'I am assuming that you are all clear on these instructions, because no one has asked for clarification'; 'Billy, please rephrase what I have just said'; 'Jenny, please explain the task for the class'. Sometimes reversing expectation can work well: 'I assume that no one understands that?'; 'Everyone unhappy?'; 'Not ready to start?' can work wonders in bringing out student questions, and does make for a touch of humour if nothing else.

Rearrange tables in your classroom, or change the seating plan to facilitate group work.	Walk around groups and 'eavesdrop' on discussions so that you can feed back good ideas to students later.	Give students question cards with question stems that they need to use during the discussion.	Model non-verbal active listening skills for students when they talk to you.
Keep your own comments to a minimum, and encourage students to build on each other's responses.	Allow students to take a plenary discussion for you, summarising the learning from the lesson.	Allow students to prepare and teach a starter activity for their peers.	Practise wrong answers with students to show them how they can move from them into learning.
Use a non-bouncy ball or soft toy—throw it to a student to start off, and that student throws it to another with each question.	Use 'phone a friend'. Let students refer tough questions to a friend for advice; they have to select which advice is useful.	Ask students to move the question up a notch—take your question and make it more challenging for the next person.	Use 'hands down' questioning for a whole lesson.
Use 'key words cards' that have to be included in answers to questions, and assign some to each table.	Ask students to use 'golden words' in their responses, which force them to develop the answer e.g. 'because...', 'therefore...'	Swap groups around by 'jigsawing' so that students work with different people in a given lesson.	Assign roles to groups so that students are obliged to participate.

Figure 7 Grid for facilitating group discussion.

Avoid rhetorical questions and empty questions

This is a basic behaviour management technique, but really should be on every teacher's watch list. Asking rhetorical questions sets you up for a negative student response, and at best makes you appear sarcastic and picky—both traits students actively dislike in teachers. Just consider for a moment the wealth of possible responses to: 'What do you think you are doing?'; 'What did you just say?'; 'What was the point of that?' and so on, and you will see that you are heading down a dead end with them all.

> ### GET WEAVING
>
> *Questions should not be wasted—make statements if you are looking for compliance rather than further interaction with the student.*

Similarly, empty questions (which are unlikely to get a response) such as: 'Who said that?'; 'Who threw that?'; 'Who doesn't understand?'; 'What are you chewing?' are unlikely to get positive or honest responses. Again, much more powerful to turn these into statements, such as: 'I asked for silence, and I can still hear talking'; 'Someone threw a piece of paper, and it needs to be picked up'; 'If you are clear about this task, please put your hand up and I will choose someone to explain it to the class'.

Don't train Barney the Wonder Horse

Clever Hans was a horse in early 20th-century Germany, a talented animal who was able to solve complex arithmetical calculations by tapping out the answer with his hoof. Investigations by the psychologist Oskar Plungst suggested that Hans was in fact responding to the unconscious cues of his trainer, and watching to see the release of tension when he reached the correct answer, so that he could stop tapping.

There is a real danger that teachers ask questions of students in this way, as though they are trying to train their own 'Clever Hans'. When I find myself doing this, I think 'Barney the Wonder Horse', and try to stop straightaway. Students can tell by your face and posture when you are pleased with their answers, or when they need to keep trying. It is really no good you telling them that they have made an 'interesting' guess or 'hmmm. . . nearly there'; they will know and keep helplessly tapping away. This is not conducive to real learning, so be aware of the cues that you give. Asking: 'Why do you think that?' or 'What evidence is there?' or asking another student to judge the answer are all ways of circumventing 'wonder horse' tendencies in your teaching.

Implement 'wait time'

Research shows that most teachers' questions are answered in less than two seconds—by the teacher. It is easy to see why—a pause of a minute can seem like a lifetime in a busy classroom, where you can feel that students will go 'off the boil' if you don't manage to keep hold of their interest all the time. But pausing before asking for an answer is really important if you are to encourage students' ability to respond to your questions.

Imagine, for instance, that you ask students to multiply 64 by 102. The moment that the first student in the class offers the answer 6528 and you applaud it as correct, the rest of the class stops calculating immediately. In that class there may be many students capable of answering that question, but they won't bother if the fastest one there always gets the credit.

Strategies to encourage wait time

Everybody wins
Try asking students to put their hands up if they think they have the correct answer, then waiting until all the class their hands up before choosing someone to respond.

Deferred reward
Wait time doesn't always have to be straight after the question. Try saying: 'In five minutes I am going to ask you...' which gets students thinking straightaway, or ask a particular student a question and tell her that you are going to ask her to give an answer in front of the class at the end of the session.

PairShare
Ask students to share their answer with the person next to them. Only after a set time do you take answers from either member of the pair.

Four to the floor
Students have to respond to the question in groups of four, and all must agree on an answer. You can then select any member of the group to offer you the group response.

Countdown

Ask students a question, then countdown from 20 to zero before you choose someone to answer. This gives students time to think, especially if you count slowly! For more excitement use a clip of the countdown clock, though be warned, the music can drive students into a frenzy of anxiety.

Phone a friend

Ask students to check their answer with the person next to them before they respond. Only if both agree can they put up their hands (this can be extended to fours, eights, a whole class if you like...).

Puppet master

Similar to 'phone a friend'. Students have to ask the person next to them for their answer and put their hand up on their behalf, then explain their partner's response. This means that students have to discuss their reasoning with each other, so it is a good way to start off class discussion.

Avoid 'hands up'

Every student teacher knows that 'hands up' is anathema—or is it? In most schools you will still find students sticking their hands up to answer questions, and teachers going along with this happily enough.

'Hands up' is so entrenched as a way of trying to get a word in edgeways that I have even resorted to it in SLT meetings, and I don't think that it's necessarily useful to get rid of it altogether. Some American research suggests that encouraging 'hands up' increases the pace of lessons and can create a positive questioning environment that encourages students from low-income households to get more involved than they would otherwise do. Anyone who has observed a lesson where the teacher gamely targets a child who has no idea what is going on will sympathise with the urge to go for the keen one at the front of the class.

However, if you wish, there are ways of avoiding it—or at least adapting it so that little Freddy and Angelina don't *always* get asked all the tricky questions.

Name and shame

The absolute favourite—know all your students by name so that you can call them out at will. I will never forget the moment a member of my department (who until then I had thought of as reasonably competent) told me that he aimed to get to know all the students' names by the end of his first term. Really? After eight weeks? Imagine how loved those students felt. Really, really, really—you need to be able to use their names as soon as humanly possible.

Learning names is tricky, I absolutely agree, but you have no excuse as a teacher—they all know yours after all. If you find it difficult to learn names (as I do), there are strategies to use, from my favourite starter (a session where they all have to learn each other's), to the old school seating-plan which you simply refer to all the time. Should students swap places without permission, ruthlessly call them the wrong names until they change back.

By the end of your first lesson with a group you will probably know the name of the most annoying child in the class, or the most disruptive, and the name of the best-behaved and keenest. Build on this, and if you learn five names thoroughly every lesson you would have them all sorted before you know it. Make sure you use names a lot, like a politician—joking apart, this really builds them into your mind—and even if this means that you find yourself saying 'So Jake, tell me Jake, how would you answer that question, Jake?' by the end of the lesson at least you will know the unfortunate child's name.

Lovely lollipops

The infamous lollipop stick strategy—write each child's name on a stick and pull them from a jar at random so as to select a student for questioning. This can be subverted by a child who steals her own stick, as famously seen on TV, and of course might result in you pulling out the children you least want to question—use at your own risk. Nothing is as tragic as a teacher fruitlessly searching through coloured lollipop sticks to aim a question at a student they could just simply target if they could let go of their AFL INSET training.

Fruit machine/student roulette

'Classtools' offer a range of random name generators, which are entertaining for students because they add that touch of thrilling gambling to the name selection. The fruit machine is one which is very popular, though my favourite is actually the roulette wheel because when it picks a name the audience cheers, which livens up questioning considerably. You can find the fruit machine on http://www.classtools. net/education-games-php/fruit_machine and the roulette wheel on http://www.classtools.net/random-name-picker/

Psychic teacher

This is my favourite, because some of my students genuinely seem baffled by my mystic powers. With this strategy, you tell students not to put their hands up, but explain that you will be able to tell who wants to answer a question by reading their mind. If you pick a few keen beans first off, they get into the swing of it, and answer fairly readily, and you can then target the shyer students, who will play along because in this instance it would be more embarrassing not to.

Anti-hands up

This works particularly well on boys who are reluctant to contribute— though I hesitate to speculate why. All you do is say that you are going to pick someone who does *not* have his or her hand up to answer the question. All hands tend to shoot up (if they don't, then follow through and pick someone without his hand up), and you can then pick someone unlikely who has his hand up 'because you look so keen'. For some reason year 9 students find this especially hysterical, and it works every time.

Explicitly teach the language of questioning

Frequently, asking classes if they have any questions is the fastest way to reduce a noisy group to stunned silence. For many students, although increasing their own use of higher-level questioning is important for developing learning, they have little sense of how to frame a higher-order question meaningfully. When asked to question somebody or something they will revert to toddler-style 'Why?' questioning which ends up being whingy and annoying.

But it's not their fault. If you don't yourself model higher-order questioning, then they won't pick it up—and if they don't know what meaningful question stems are like, then they will find it very difficult to create their own questions.

I like to use question cards or question speech bubbles—speech bubbles for classroom display, cards for everyday use. With the cards (oh the magic of lamination!) you can hand them out to students and explain that they have to use the question at some time during the lesson—once they've done this they can hand it back to you. Each student gets several cards, according to ability, throughout the lesson. This helps to avoid questioning being dominated by a few confident students, creates a variety of questioning, and allows you to embed more sophisticated questioning practice in the class.

If you try this with students, at first they may tend to be sulky, and be delighted if they get a 'get out of jail free'-style question such as: 'Where are we in this discussion?' However, if you keep using the cards, after a while you will see them start to ask to swap question cards, as the questioning becomes less mechanical. Finally they will ask if they can frame their own questions, and your job is done.

Understand why you are asking questions, and use them deliberately

Using the same kind of question stems that you can offer students, you can make sure that you practise deeper questioning, which will encourage students to re-think and reinvestigate their own presuppositions. They fall into the following categories:

Clarification

These questions try to make students make their ideas clear, and firm up their concepts—in other words, they ask them to reflect on what they are thinking about. They encourage students to explain and define terms, and to give examples.

- Can you explain that?
- Can you give me an example?
- Can you rephrase that?
- How does this connect with what we've been talking about?

- What do we already know about this?
- What exactly does this mean?
- Why are you saying that?

Presuppositions

These questions ask students to reflect on why they have certain presuppositions—what the beliefs are with which they are working, and whether these assumptions are justified or reasonable.

- Can you justify your opinion?
- Can you give me an example of that?
- How do you know this?
- How might someone object to this?
- On what authority do you base your argument?
- What are your reasons?
- What evidence is there to support what you are saying?
- What is the nature of this?
- Would it stand up in court?

Alternative views

These questions move on from the former ones to consider different ways of thinking, asking students to consider other people's viewpoints.

- Can you put it another way?
- How else could we approach this?
- Is there another point of view?
- What alternative ways of looking at this are there?
- What are the strengths and weaknesses of your idea?
- What else could we assume?
- What would someone who disagreed with you say?
- Who benefits from this?

Consequences

These questions ask students to consider the consequences of their argument, and try and predict its implications (this is also a good way to anticipate objections in debate, or see the other side of the story).

- Then what would happen?
- What are the consequences of that assumption?
- How does this fit with what we learned before?
- Why is this important?
- What follows from what you say?
- What can we work out from this?
- Does that view agree with what was said earlier?
- What would be the consequences of that?
- Is there a general rule for that?
- How would you test to see if that was true?

Questioning the question

These questions reflect ideas back to the students, and ask them to reflect on why questions are asked at the outset. Good for re-starting a discussion, or moving it into another area.

- Are we any closer to answering our question?
- Can someone summarise our progress so far?
- How could you rephrase that question?
- Is that the best way to ask that question?
- What are you trying to achieve?
- What other ways would there be of asking that?
- What should we change about how we discuss this issue?
- What was the point of asking that question?
- Where have we got to with our discussion?
- Why do you think I asked this question?

Use plenary questions

At the end of a lesson, plenary questions are invaluable for checking how students have investigated a task, and for considering how you might tweak that task another time. I like to use a set of Andy Brumby-inspired plenary question cards (see Figure 8), which I can either use to prompt my own questions or else hand out to students (almost) at random:

What are the advantages and disadvantages of working in this way?	What advice would you give to someone who wants to understand what we learned today?	If I were planning to teach this lesson to another group, would you advise me to change anything?	Who contributed most to your group's final outcome, and how can you tell?
Which person has helped you to make progress in today's lesson? Why?	What would a good outcome for this learning objective look like? Have you achieved it?	What learning strategy has helped you to make progress in today's lesson? Why?	What emotions have you experienced during today's lesson? Which were most helpful for learning?
How has your thinking about this topic changed since the beginning of the lesson?	What was your best and/or worst decision in class today and how did it affect your learning?	What was it that best helped you to understand how to achieve the success criteria?	Which of the resources we used today is most valuable for learning about the objective, and why?
Where else could you use the skill you used today, and in what circumstances?	What was unexpected about today's lesson, and how did this help you to learn?	What different learning styles have you tried during today's lesson? Which were most helpful for learning?	Where have you made improvements to your work in response to feedback?
How could someone prove that they have achieved today's learning objective?	Which part of the lesson did you most enjoy, and why?	What feedback today was most helpful? Why?	What has been the most interesting question anyone has asked today? Why?

Figure 8 Plenary question cards prompt teacher questions.

If you question students about the processes of their own learning, you will soon find that they will be more confident about working independently. You will also garner invaluable information about how the students like to learn, and which learning styles they find most comfortable. Ultimately, making students independent learners (sometimes seen as the Holy Grail of teaching) means that you have to let them reproduce some of the processes of your own learning.

Letting students investigate for themselves makes them both independent and more confident—and though it may be more trouble to set up and plan, once these habits are established, lessons will virtually run themselves. Having students who can openly discuss with adults how and why they are learning not only means that you have people to help you explain what you are doing if you should be observed, but also means that you quickly get students who are actually interested in what you have to teach, who can genuinely advise you, and who become partners in their own learning.

4

Differentiation: Teaching Right to the Edge

*Everybody is a genius. But if you judge a fish by its ability to climb a tree,
it will live its whole life believing that it is stupid.*
(Albert Einstein)

Teacher 1: I've taught my dog to talk!

Teacher 2: Amazing—what can he say?

Teacher 1: I said I'd taught him—I didn't say he'd learned to do it.

Embedding differentiation in the classroom

Differentiation is crucial for an outstanding lesson. It is one of the things that you notice immediately as an observer, one of the things that OFSTED looks for so as to make sure that you are helping each student to make progress. It doesn't matter if you have a high-ability group or the bottom set, they can make progress, and how well you differentiate is the key to that.

For me, differentiation includes behaviour management, because managing behaviour appropriately is one of the ways in which you provide for each child's needs. As Sue Cowley puts it, the typical teacher, pitching a lesson at the average student, 'gets it exactly right for only one third of the class', which makes it hardly surprising that the other two-thirds may then misbehave.

When observing lessons, it is easy to see how the off-task students tend to be those for whom the work is too easy or too difficult. Students with weak literacy skills, for instance, will use avoidance tactics to distract from their own difficulties, and make the teacher focus on their behaviour rather than on their learning. Brighter students who have finished work quickly will often engage in attention-seeking behaviour while they are waiting for the teacher to notice. For this reason, this chapter will cover both behaviour management strategies and traditional differentiation.

Managing behaviour effectively

Really effective differentiation provides for those learning needs that are less obvious than not being able to add 2 + 2. If a child is unable to learn in your classroom because the work is too hard, that is, of course your responsibility. However, if a child is unable to learn because they are engaged in low-level distraction, or because others are also engaged in low-level distraction, then teaching effective working habits is also your responsibility.

Creating firm boundaries

As with very small children, school students need to have effective and consistent boundaries to their behaviour. This does not mean that you are inflexible—quite the reverse. Students need to see you as 'strict-but-fair', a teacher who is capable of relaxing the rules when it is appropriate, but who is otherwise consistent and reasonable.

Have a seating plan

Always, always have a seating plan. What the plan is like doesn't much matter, but it is important that you are in charge of where people sit, and that students know that. Telling students where to sit is one of the first signs for them that you are in control of the class, and they will like the sense of order it brings. Incidentally, if you have a student who tends to resist instruction, start off by asking them to do something that they like doing—such as open a window for you. This will then unconsciously set up in their mind that you are someone to be obeyed, and that doing what you say is not difficult or unpleasant.

GET WEAVING

When you are getting to know a new class, try using class photos stuck on an A3 sheet as your seating plan to make sure you match names and faces quickly.

Shared seating plans across subjects are especially effective for challenging groups. If students know who they will be working with, even in differently designed classrooms, groups tend to become more stable. In this case, as in so many cases, knowing the class better, so as to differentiate effectively, is the starting-point for change.

Never shout

If you wish your students to respect you, never shout. It is the one thing that students dislike more than anything else, and it is the one thing that signals to them that you are out of control, and that you are therefore not consistent. Of course you may find at times that you need to raise and project your voice to be heard when calling for attention, but it can be more helpful to use a non-verbal signal for this. Holding up your hand feels counter-intuitive, but works well (many primary schools use this strategy, so students are sometimes already trained to respond to it), or you could try holding up something else—I used to use a conch shell when I was teaching *Lord of the Flies,* which had the added bonus of reminding them of a key point in the book.

Other non-verbal signals for silence include switching the lights on or off (works especially well in winter), using a bell or a buzzer as a signal for students to look to the front, or the countdown clock (which can be readily found on YouTube). Another successful strategy is playing music in the classroom as students enter, turning it up loud enough to drown out student chatter, before turning it down quickly—then speaking in the sudden silence.

Resist the temptation to talk over students. They won't listen properly. If you want to say something—and you should, with a chatty class, try and make sure that your lesson is designed so that you are not making them be silent every five minutes—then it is important, and students need to be silent so that they may hear it. It is really worth getting them into this good habit early on so that you don't have to do it every lesson. Wait for silence, even if it takes a while. With a very vocal class, count down from 5 to zero, signalling as you go:

'Five. . .it's time to stop talking. . .
Four. . .finish your sentence. . .
Three. . .time to put your pens down. . .
Two. . .looking my way. . .
One. . .even you, Jack. . .
Zero. . .everybody ready?'

If students are resistant to the countdown for silence, then for every second they keep talking make a mark on the board, which translates into time at the end of the lesson. This can be time out of break, if your lesson is before break or at the end of the day, or simply time spent standing silently after clearing up at the end of the lesson. Call for clear up five minutes earlier than you need, and I can guarantee that students will not want to repeat the dragging minutes as they wait for you to let them go.

A refinement of this strategy (which I prefer, as it is never good to punish the whole class for the misdemeanours of a few) is to note who is actually talking and note their names down, again with marks for repetition of the offence. This then means that you can let the compliant students go first, and keep those who were talking over you until last, in a graduated fashion. I generally then take the opportunity to ask those left last why they think they are last to go—and have a brief discussion about wasting people's time. They quickly get the point.

When you do get to talk, keep it brief, and make sure you have a reason for speech. Give instructions clearly. Use strong, large signals. Project your voice clearly, slow down as you are speaking, emphasise key words.

Avoid 'because I say so'

Children love to argue the toss—again, like toddlers. Denying them the opportunity to do this is about as effective as saying 'because I say so'. Closing down debate is never a good management strategy, because it sends the message that you have no real reason for what you do. What you need to do here is build up a system of rational arguments to which you can refer, and refer to them all the time.

Some schools have an existing behaviour management policy that you can refer to, such as LEARN, where each letter stands for a type of behaviour considered desirable. Because students are used to all teachers referring to this policy, quick reference to it can rapidly prevent arguments. However, if you do not have such a policy in place, you will need to devise your own set of quick rationalisations for each behaviour issue that you have to deal with. You then simply repeat these all the time until students become bored with asking why. For instance:

TEACHER: Please stop talking.

STUDENT: But I wasn't. . .

TEACHER: When you talk, you distract others.

STUDENT: But I was talking about the work.

TEACHER: When you talk while I am talking, you distract others from what I am saying.

STUDENT: But I was helping. . .

TEACHER: If you're not sure about my reasons, we can discuss it at the end of the lesson.

It is often difficult when a student has a point, as in this case—their interruption had a purpose—but you still need to get on with the lesson, and they still need to know when to stay silent. Because you use the same words and ideas each time someone interrupts, students wanting personal attention stop interrupting, because it is less satisfying. You can then offer to discuss the issue with a student at break time or after the lesson. I have often found that an invitation like this will often result in compliance without further argument—though if the student does turn up, you can have a useful conversation with her.

Be consistent

One thing that students often complain about is teachers who seem to have favourites or who are in good or bad moods. Always try and be consistent in your classroom so that students know that the same behaviour will have the same consequences. If you are in a situation where you really don't want to sanction a child who is normally good, then make it clear to the others how they have earned that good behaviour, and offer them the same reward, e.g. 'Jack is going to escape a homework detention because he has brought in every piece of homework on time this term, and will therefore have an extension until tomorrow. Is anyone else in that situation?'

In the same way, check carefully your interactions with each student in a class. I once had to deal with a parent who claimed that a particular member of staff had literally never spoken to her child. The teacher in question wasn't absolutely sure this wasn't the case. Good practice in questioning will help with this. I like to have a mark sheet in front of me to monitor my initial interactions with a class, where I tick a child's name whenever I speak to him or her. Very rapidly, using this, you can see the pattern of attention in the group, and who is getting—or demanding—the most from you. You can then adjust accordingly, depending on any bias you observe. One easy way to do this is to take the register by marking in a child once you have spoken to them— again you will rapidly notice if people are flying under the radar.

Sincerity comes later

Students who misbehave will often try to draw you into 'secondary behaviour'. All this means is that you start off asking a student to sit down (the primary behaviour you are trying to address) and end up having a raging argument with him about his tone of voice (the secondary behaviour he is using to distract you). Adolescents can be particularly skilled at saying something in what sounds like an insolent way, or raising their eyebrows or rolling their eyes at your instructions.

Avoid at all costs getting drawn into secondary behaviour. The very fact that students are using it is a tribute to the fact that you are making them comply with your instructions. If they have, for instance, apologised to another student for calling them something unpleasant, and you then demand that they repeat the apology using a sincere tone of voice, you are on a losing wicket—sincerity comes later. For the moment the words are enough, and any small bit of self-esteem that they can claw back by acting out is fine. If you remain calm, it will be clear that you have won the battle. More than that—it should not be about winning a battle. You are the adult.

Speak carefully

Whatever you say to students is a model for them—so watch how you speak. It should go without saying that you do not yourself swear in the classroom or around the school within students' earshot (though I have known teachers who do), and you should also try and use formal language and not slang wherever possible. Speaking carefully to students gives them dignity, reminds them that you are a professional, and can have a marked effect on their behaviour.

Handsome is as handsome does

Courtesy is key to creating a good atmosphere in your classroom. Learn students' names as fast as you can, and then use them as much as you can, to build up a sense that you really know who they are. Remember, they all know who you are. If you use someone's name, it adds a great deal of power to your instructions, and it is a good way of calling attention to the fact that you have your eye on them. Don't always use names to pick out the non-compliant student, though—thank students who get on with things quickly. If you ask students to get their books out, for instance, following this up with 'thank you, Casey, thank you, Kyla' your words instantly signal to the others that they may get praised if they do the same—and praise is a powerful tool.

> ## GET WEAVING
>
> *Hold to the same standards outside your classroom as you do inside. If you are inconsistent about picking up on student behaviour in corridors or playgrounds, they will be slower to respond to you in lessons.*

Always greet students with a smile and a pleasant comment. If they happen to hold the door for you, thank them for their courtesy. If they drop something, try picking it up for them—it will mean that they will be far more likely to imitate you. Emphasise that in your classroom certain rules apply—the implication is that it doesn't matter what goes on elsewhere, you have the highest standards. 'In this classroom we speak politely to each other' may sound wishful thinking the first time you say it, but will become fact the more you enforce it.

Use neutral language

Wherever possible with students, try and use neutral language. Once you bring your own personality into a reprimand, that becomes a chink through which they can try and attack you. Students are looking for boundaries, but they will seek to push these where they can. In the classroom, teachers need to be like ideal parents, in that it should not be possible for students to make them angry. Of course you may become angry or frustrated by a child's behaviour, but it is essential that you do not show this and remain calm.

Using neutral language not only helps with dealing with your own feelings—because it takes the personal out of the situation—but also focuses attention on behaviour rather than on the child. Many students who manifest with behavioural difficulties are particularly challenging to adults, and need a calm manner so that they do not feel attacked. Just imagine if you had had a row with your family, drove to work and got stuck in a traffic jam, rushed across the car park to get to your morning meeting and the first words that you heard were 'you're late'. It would hardly help your mood. It is the same for children. Using a neutral statement gives a child space to explain what has happened to them, and avoids the problem of reprimanding a child for something that they didn't do, or for which they have a good excuse. Neutral statements also remove the 'logic gap' where students will rush in to object to what you say.

When you first try neutralising your language you are likely to think that it sounds really artificial and odd—but trust me, it is worth persisting. To neutralise you must focus on facts and observations, and avoid personal comments that students will often interpret as accusations. Eventually students themselves will pick up the language you use and the calmness will diffuse itself throughout the classroom.

The table below gives some examples of how to neutralise language:

Table 4 How to use neutral language with students.

Instead of saying	Which invites the response	Try saying
You're late.	No, I'm not; I fell off my bike. . .	The lesson started at 9 a.m. and it is now 9.10.
You're talking.	I was just explaining. . .	I asked for quiet and I can still hear voices.
Stop chewing gum.	It's not gum, it's. . .	You are chewing something and you need to get rid of that (offer bin).
Stop listening to your headphones.	They're not switched on. . .	Wearing headphones distracts from learning and is against the rules.
Who threw that paper on the floor?	Not me—I'm not touching it. . .	There is paper on the floor, and it will need to be put in the bin before the class can leave.
How dare you use that language?	No problem, Miss—I do it all the time. . .	The language just used is inappropriate for this classroom. If I hear it again, I will have to assume that you are being deliberately rude.
What did you say?	Nothing. . .	I heard language which is inappropriate for the classroom. If I hear it again, I will have to assume that you are being deliberately rude.
Stop rocking on your chair.	I wasn't. . .	All four legs of the chair need to be in contact with the floor.

Using neutral language does take a little practice, but it is a really useful tool for behaviour management.

Jumping record

You are probably familiar with the 'stuck record' strategy, where you simply repeat your instructions until they are followed. It is certainly helpful when trying to establish boundaries. However, when students are misbehaving, simply repeating your instructions with no great emotion will not always have much of an impact. I prefer the 'jumping record' strategy, where you repeat your instructions in the same fashion as the 'stuck record', but each time you add something, such as the student's name, to add extra emphasis to the repetition. This surprisingly often results in obedience. For example:

TEACHER: Please sit down.

STUDENT: But I was just going to...

TEACHER: Please sit down (Name).

STUDENT: I will in a minute, but...

TEACHER: (Name), you need to sit down.

STUDENT: But that's unfair, I just...

TEACHER: (Name), you need to sit down now.

STUDENT: [sits down]

Manage your own behaviour

You are actually the most important person in a classroom, because your behaviour makes a huge impact on the class. The way you feel and act will model behaviour for the class, and your positive energy and confidence will translate into confidence for them about their learning. It is really hard to stay grumpy in the face of someone who believes in you.

Stay smiling

Of course there will be times when you do not feel happy in school, and times when you are tempted to bring home troubles to work. Avoid this at all costs, and get into the habit of having a cheerful work persona. I often really exaggerate cheerfulness when coming into school (and on gate duty) and this makes people laugh, which correspondingly tends to cheer me up. If you smile, you do actually feel better (something to do with creating endorphins) even if it feels artificial at first.

Make sure that you have some people you can talk to, or some element of a routine—something that calms you and makes you feel upbeat. I tend to play particular music on the way to work, for instance, which puts me in a good mood, and I make time for a cup of coffee before I start. Always think of something good that is going to happen that day, and focus on it.

GET WEAVING

Make sure that for lessons that you anticipate will be challenging that you use enjoyable resources. For instance, consider showing video clips, or having some 'hands on' making and doing.

If you have a class which you find especially challenging, it is really important that you do not let them know that you fear and dread their lessons—imagine if you had a meeting with someone who hated meeting with you. Of course you would be able to tell, and so can students. Instead, give yourself some little reward every time you teach them or turn a negative into a positive in your mind so that (for instance) the fact that you have them last lesson on a Friday means that once it's over you have a weekend to look forward to. If I have a difficult lesson in prospect, I tend to come into it and say: 'Do you know, I've been looking forward to this lesson *all day*?' which has the merit of being true, and makes a huge difference to student attitude. They instantly want to know why—and feel better for thinking that you actually like them and want to teach them. Hopefully you will have thought of some little surprise to make it true.

Remember that you are the grown-up

Perilously easy to forget, but always remember that even large and stroppy adolescents are children—and may often be frightened children. I remember being startled by meeting a particularly difficult student's father at parents' evening—I found his manner terrifying, and realised immediately that the student concerned was reacting to, and imitating, his father's behaviour. I became resolved to give him a better role-model for adult behaviour by staying calm and 'grown-up', no matter what the provocation, and it worked well.

Students who have difficulties with work in school can often be especially skilled at winding up adults—something they may have practised a great deal—so you may need strategies to remind yourself in moments of stress that you need to avoid being led into confrontation. I used to pretend that I was being filmed for a documentary (amazing how this adds to the length of time one can speak patiently) or being observed. I also like to imagine differential pay. Some of my classes are more challenging than others, and I imagine that for these classes

I am paid a great deal, whereas for the more pleasant ones I am paid much less. It sounds childish, but it does help at the end of a long day to consider that whereas you are being paid to be in the lesson, and ultimately have a choice whether you can remain, the children you teach are actually compelled by law to attend school, and don't get paid a penny. Anything to keep that smile on your face!

Managing work effectively

In *Students Who Drive You Crazy* Kottler gives a long list of possible reasons for difficult behaviour, focusing on the ways in which children respond negatively to certain stimuli. Nearly all of the reasons he names, such as boredom and frustration, concern issues that can be solved through effective differentiation of student work.

I don't think that I have ever observed bad behaviour in a classroom where the differentiation of the lesson was perfect, though this may be because good differentiation implies that the teacher knows the class inside-out. Where tasks are personalised for students, and the teacher has thought carefully about each student and his or her experience of learning, behaviour management generally ceases to be an issue, because the reasons for bad behaviour are reduced or removed. In a well-differentiated lesson, not only are opportunities for difficult behaviour fewer, but students are simply too busy and engaged to think up avoidance strategies. So, differentiating effectively is immensely rewarding for the teacher, as well as for the students. It may seem time-consuming as a project, but taken bit by bit, each part of differentiation will add up to a whole which is sustainable and practicable, not just in individual classrooms, but for the whole school.

Create a class profile

It may sound like a truism, but if you do not know your students, it is impossible to differentiate properly for them. Knowing students means far more than getting their names right (though that is a start!); it means having a real sense of how they work together as a group, where the pinch points lie, and how the dynamics of their relationships will affect your attempts to differentiate the work. Once you have all the information, record it in an easy-to-understand form, not just in your mark book, but in a folder that you can use when planning for this specific group.

If you have a class profile folder, it should contain within it student details such as a register, a copy of class photos, a copy of your seating plan, and your notes on individual students. Kept in a secure place, it becomes a record which you can use not only for yourself, but for anyone else who teaches that class. If you should be away, and a cover teacher is there, you can put the cover instructions into this folder, and the teacher will instantly have a much clearer idea of how to treat the class, and how to teach them effectively.

GET WEAVING

Find out one individual fact about each of your students—it can be that they are left handed, have two older sisters, their favourite sport—almost anything will do, though it's best if it means something to them. You can then use this to personalise the class, and make a point of contact through which to get to know your students.

Locating information

It can be worth giving a class a 'fresh start' feeling and not letting them know how well you know them—for disaffected students, in particular, this can really help them feel that they can start afresh with you—but it is absolutely essential that you do make sure that you have tracked down every piece of information on the school system about your students. If something is not readily available, then ask until you find it, and then ask why you couldn't find it—if it's not easy for you, it will not be easy for other teachers to find, especially new teachers to the school, or NQTs or trainees.

Don't limit yourself to the obvious SEN (Special Educational Needs) details of SA (School Action) and SA+ (School Action Plus); check out (for instance) if a student in your class has suffered bereavement, and if so, when the anniversary comes. Find out if she has older and younger siblings, and what their experience of school has been so far. Has she been in trouble at school before you taught her? What are her pressure points?

Making sense of information

It is no good having a list of ticks or Ys in a column telling you that a child is gifted or EAL (English as an Additional Language) or SA or anything else—you need to translate that material for your class profile. This can be as simple as creating another column in your existing documents, and incorporating all the information into a sentence or two. Thus simple ticks can transfer into: 'This student has English as an additional language; her first language is Portuguese. She has a sibling in year 11, and came to the school last year with little English. She is young for the year, with an August birthday'. Writing out the facts like this is important, as it makes the particulars real to you. By constructing a sentence, you will be forced to think about which aspects of the information link together, and which might have an effect upon each other. It's the first step towards differentiation.

Once you get to know the students better, you will be able to add more personal notes to these rough outlines. Think carefully. If there are standard problems, there should be standard solutions. If a child is dyslexic for instance, there should be some indication of your awareness of this issue, and some accommodation for it in every lesson you plan involving this child—even if all it is, is the use of a particular colour of paper for handouts, or a particular font that makes text easier to access for that child. A good rule of thumb is to consider—if you were suddenly unable to teach the class, would another teacher, from your notes, be able to effectively differentiate? The answer should always be 'yes'.

Once you have created a class profile, make sure that your seating plan reflects this information. My school currently shares with teachers a simple Excel database which allows teachers to 'drop down' the information on SIMS (School Information Management System) into a colour-coded seating plan, which has by each student's name his current levels, predicted levels, special educational needs and other notes the teacher may wish to include. It is a good reminder to use when constructing seating plans, and it also makes visible to any observer the rationale for the seating plan. This sort of colour-coding is also useful for making it clear to you why some students will work well together. Whatever your reasons for seating students next to each other, they will have something to do with differentiation, and it is as well to make this reasoning clear to yourself as well as to any visitor to your classroom.

Consider reading ages

When differentiating, it can be easy to forget the useful information carried by reading ages. I have known members of staff who have dutifully recorded a low reading age on a pupil profile, and then blithely given said student the same worksheet as the rest of the class. This is clearly setting up the child concerned for problems before you even start the lesson.

Fortunately, in Microsoft Word the spelling and grammar check contains an option to show readability statistics. Click on the spelling and grammar check, and ensure that this option is ticked, and then once you have created a worksheet, you can check it for spelling and grammar, and at the end of the check it should show readability statistics in a pop-up box, like so (the example shown is for part of the text of this chapter). This helpfully gives the number of passive sentences (in general, active sentences are easier for students to read) and also gives a grade score. As this is designed for American schools, simply add 5 to the score to get a reading age.

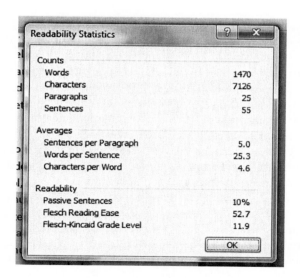

Figure 9 The grammar check in Microsoft Word showing the readability of a text.

This check shows that the text of this chapter, you will note, is suitable for adults—so I would have to rewrite it substantially to make it accessible for a school audience. Fleisch reading ease is calculated from 1–100, and the higher the score the more readable is the text. A text for an average GCSE student should be between 60 and 80. Again the score of this chapter is too low to be useful to a school reader. It is worthwhile getting used to the kind of texts accessible for different readers. In particular, if you have students with low reading ages in your classroom, you will need to get used to knowing what a text designed for such a reading age looks like, and create your worksheets accordingly.

An even simpler way of checking readability is to use an online tool such as http://www.read-able.com/ where you can cut and paste a web address to find if a website is accessible, or paste text directly into a box to have it evaluated with a useful red/amber/green system of bars to show readability. Once you do this a few times, it becomes clear what you need to change, and you will find that the shifts become more and more second nature. Don't just use this to accommodate weaker students—try and raise the sophistication of worksheets to stretch the more able, or offer them texts which are just slightly out of their reading comfort zone to add extra challenge to a lesson.

Generally, long sentences and complex vocabulary will increase the reading age of a text. To reverse this, then, use short sentences, and simpler language. If you look at the simple English Wikipedia, http://simple.wikipedia.org/wiki/Main_Page, this will give you some idea of the kind of language that is accessible. Alternately, ask your librarian to share with you children's books suitable for the reading ages you are trying to access. Looking at the language of *The Gruffalo*, for instance, is a quick way of recalibrating your expectations.

To lower the reading age of texts you want to use in class, repeat key words, use bullet points to break up the text, use diagrams and pictures to illustrate ideas, and try and make worksheets visually appealing. This kind of differentiation may seem time-consuming, but once done, it is done for future classes, and you may find that you can get your TA or someone else working centrally in the department to adapt worksheets for you as well.

Use key words

Another aspect of literacy that you will need to focus on when differentiating is the use of key words and command words for students. Always make sure that students are familiar with the kind of key words and command words that they will find in an exam. Although at first these words may seem complex and difficult for students to access, using word cards, word walls, spelling tests, and other strategies can soon make them familiar.

GET WEAVING

Notice the spellings which students consistently get wrong, and use them as the basis for whole-class spelling tests. A once-a-week homework of a spelling test is easy to mark and track.

It is not helpful to always use simpler versions of assessment objectives or questions to help students who struggle with reading; sometimes you simply need to equip them with the appropriate language for the subject or topic. Highlighting where these words turn up on exam papers or test papers can make for an engaging display and helps desensitise children to complex exam language.

This kind of differentiation can be embedded in whole-school strategy, as at my current school, where the 'word of the day' is a word taken from the academic word list, and students get credits for using the word appropriately during the day in speech or writing. This allows teachers to employ these words in tutorial activities as well as lessons, and reduces the amount of planning teachers need to do for differentiation, as they can use the assigned words, knowing that they will form part of a systematic plan. However, if your school does not run a similar scheme, then try using the academic word list yourself to supply students with appropriate vocabulary.

The very useful University of Nottingham website http://www.nottingham.ac.uk/alzsh3/acvocab/index.htm not only gives you the academic word list and its rationale, but also provides tools for using it, for instance a tool that will highlight key words from the list in a given text—a useful exercise to try when differentiating for a group. It also has exercises where students can learn words through gap-filling or quizzes, which you may find helpful to help reinforce key words for students.

If you need to focus on particular key words, this should be done gradually—even one or two at a time—always making sure that new language is introduced at appropriate times and that you explain and add it to a glossary as students encounter it for the first time. Students have a remarkable capacity to memorise words that they see frequently, so using them as a key part of displays will also help students to absorb the language into their own register. Using 'literacy mats', as many schools now do (with basic literacy reminders on one side and subject-specific key words and concepts on the other) is a straightforward way of doing this, and is another way of targeting differentiation, with different mats used to support different groups of students.

Set a range of tasks

Giving students a choice of tasks and a choice of levels is important for differentiation. At the simplest, using the language of choice, as in 'must/ should/ could', is a useful starting-point, which at least helps to demonstrate that there are different ways of approaching a piece of learning. For really effective differentiation, though, creating choice is not enough in itself—you need to make sure that the choices concerned are sufficiently different from each other, and represent real challenges.

Use Bloom's taxonomy for task-setting

Make sure that tasks for differentiation do not simply ask students to do more of a thing, but invite them to try something that is inherently more advanced in thinking terms. Using Bloom's can be helpful here, to remind yourself how, for instance, students might move from understanding key facts to then applying that knowledge. You can use Bloom's prompts to help you devise extension tasks that are creative and so act as a real reward for those who have finished work early. Table 5 gives the Bloom's levels with some matching task key words and examples.

Table 5 Matching task key words and examples to Bloom's taxonomy.

Level of Bloom's	Sample task	Key words
Knowledge	• Match the key words with the definitions. • Identify and label pictures.	*List, define, tell, label, identify, state*
Comprehension	• Categorise quotations into groups depending on theme. • Sort animals into predators and prey animals.	*Describe, name, identify, discuss, explain, organise*
Application	• Construct a database for a shop which tracks profit and loss. • Annotate a CD holder design to indicate its suitability for purpose.	*Modify, solve, change, explain, show, examine*
Analysis	• Select quotations to illustrate a particular viewpoint. • Compare two sources and determine their points of agreement.	*Analyse, separate, compare, contrast, investigate, outline*
Synthesis	• Plan and design a habitat that is suitable for keeping corn-snakes in captivity. • Answer hot-seating questions in character as Antigone.	*Create, construct, plan, role-play, design, formulate, propose, imagine*
Evaluation	• Set up a court room in which George is accused of the murder of Lennie, and play prosecution and defence roles, using evidence from the text. • Evaluate the most suitable experiment to determine whether chemical reactions lose mass.	*Give opinion, criticise, discriminate, summarise, argue, debate, justify*

Use different learning styles

Considering different learning styles can be really helpful when devising differentiated tasks. This is not just to try and accommodate students' preferred learning styles, but to prevent them (and you) from falling into a rut where one type of learning is prioritised over another. Teachers, by the very nature of their training, tend to be highly literate, and if you are not careful, you can find that you rely heavily upon worksheets, for instance, when some of your students would benefit from a more practical approach.

A helpful way of planning for differentiation, then, is to consider if you are using a sufficient variety of ways to access learning in each lesson. Giving students a choice means that they will be more patient with the forms of learning that they find difficult because they will know that there will be something else that they find easier to engage with. If in every class there is a tactile activity, an activity that encourages discussion, some individual interaction with the teacher, a visual stimulus, a written stimulus and a creative stimulus, classes rarely get dull. They move faster for teacher and student alike.

Images or objects are a good way in to devising more creative styles of learning, as they encourage critical thinking. Images have no reading ages. One of the problems with students who have low literacy is that they can be frustrated by tasks that are too simple for their cognitive age. Allowing them to take the lead in a picture-based discussion will give them the confidence that they need to work on literacy in another part of the lesson. Try asking students to relate a series of images to a concept—to choose the most apt illustrations for an article, for instance—and in this way get them discussing conceptual issues as well as details of fact.

Try using the 'give me five' principle with tasks, so that groups are working in different ways for the same purpose. This avoids the problems of students simply copying each other, but also encourages them to help each other in more productive ways. Jigsawing students works in a similar way, when they initially work on the same aspect of a task, and then split into different groups so that they have to teach what they have discovered to other groups.

Targets and checks

When you differentiate tasks, you should run them through in your head to consider how they will be responded to by different types of student. How will a lazy but able student respond? How will a student who is easily distracted respond? This is where the class profile is essential. Students need to be regularly checked during the lesson to make sure that they are working at tasks that are sufficiently challenging for their abilities, and they need to reflect on their own choice of tasks so that they are aware when they are not challenging themselves sufficiently.

One strategy for achieving this is to build in regular checks to the lesson, so that students can let you know quickly if they are struggling. The RAG (red, amber and green traffic light method) is a familiar strategy which you can extend to help with this situation in different ways. Getting students to RAG a series of skills quickly shows you where they feel confident, and you can reinforce levels of challenge by making them match so that students have red, amber and green targets.

Having a red, amber and green page on a planner, similarly, can allow students to turn to the relevant page and place it face-upwards on their desks so that the teacher can quickly survey the room and see where students see themselves as confident or struggling with a given task. Thumbs up and thumbs down can also work as a quick check (though the accuracy of this can sometimes be adversely affected by peer pressure—even unconsciously).

Another tool to use is 'agree/disagree' cards. Put on the board a statement such as: 'I am happy with the work I am doing and understand what I need to do', then ask students to adjust the cards on their tables to respond to the statement accordingly. This allows students to ask for help without making themselves conspicuous with their peers, and means that you can quickly scan the classroom to see where students need extra support.

One good aspect of this system is that you can change the statement, so that students might, for instance, have to agree or disagree with the idea 'I am finding this work a challenge'. Establishing what students already understand before you start the lesson will help you work out where on the differentiation continuum you will need to start.

Question carefully

Questioning is key to successful differentiation. If you question effectively, you can challenge students and support them simply by varying the type of questioning. Asking more able students to justify their ideas, or compare them to others, or to extend or exemplify someone else's response, is a very direct way of addressing their individual learning needs. It's important to remember and revisit the basics of questioning: using 'wait time'; having a mixture of 'hands up' and 'hands down' questioning; 'bouncing' questions around the class so that the questioning avoids the 'question/answer/approval' exchange.

It is easy to forget, however, that creating questions and asking them is just as important for students as being asked questions. Make sure that your students are taught the language of questioning so that they start to understand the processes of their own learning. I explain to all my classes the difference between higher and lower-order questions by using the analogy of Dr Watson (lower-order, closed questions) and Sherlock Holmes (higher-order, open questions) so that they are aware of how they can themselves develop questioning in a discussion. Question cards can help students to use this language more consciously; this strategy offers a supporting framework for developing questioning.

Once students are aware of different questioning levels, use 'blooming circles' (see Chapter 3) where students answer a series of questions that circle round a central image or piece of text. The questions gradually get harder, but students can choose where they start. This freedom of choice seems to encourage students to become more adventurous and challenge themselves—something about the circular structure also invites them in more powerfully than a list of questions that get harder as they progress.

Also successful has been a related activity, where students have to create a sequence of questions on the same principles. Given a snippet of text or an image or a proposition, they have to try and imitate the Bloom structure, with or without prompts, depending on how well they know it, so as to create a circle of questions. In order to think of the questions, of course, they have to consider the possible answers. Thinking of how to make up more challenging questions encourages them to investigate a concept or a text more closely—and these can then be exchanged with other students and answered.

Watch other teachers

Other teachers can be your strongest allies when it comes to differentiating effectively for a class. At the start of the school year, if you have not taught a class before, try and speak to the class's previous teacher. It is likely that the teacher will immediately zone in on the students who have differentiation issues, as they are likely to be the ones who have also had behavioural issues. This does not have to be a long interview. Simply ask the previous teacher about the class and record what he says with a mini voice recorder or on your phone, if you do not have time to take notes—this record gives you a starting-point, but if you keep it, this will become even more useful as you get to know the group yourself.

If you have taught the class already, and feel that you know the students, but don't have a complete handle on them in terms of effective differentiation, try and observe them with another teacher in a different subject—or simply compare notes in the staffroom. Talking through how a class appears in another subject for a different teacher can be immensely illuminating, and will give you a different perspective on their skills and abilities.

If you watch your students with another teacher, this does not always have to mean a formal observation, but can involve simply popping in for ten minutes to see how a lesson starts or ends, or coming in to watch a specific task or piece of group work. Watching other subjects can give you fresh ideas for your own practice, ranging from seating plans to different types of worksheet and more kinaesthetic tasks.

Effective differentiation means that your classes may seem like more work to plan, but that they will go better once you are in the lesson. Once you get into the habit of devising different styles of task, students will start to expect these, and you should find that they become more eager and interested to learn. Ultimately, all that successful differentiation seeks to do is to make sure that no one in the lesson is bewildered—including you—and that no one has time on his or her hands and is uncertain what to do with it—including you. Well worth the trouble.

5

Evaluation: Weighing the Pig Properly

Spoon feeding in the long run teaches us nothing
but the shape of the spoon.
(E.M. Forster)

Of course, weighing the pig doesn't make it fatter, but acting on the data (i.e. altering the pig's diet) could well make it fatter. It's certainly more likely that the farmer weighing the pig will be able to take action to fatten his/her pig, whereas the farmer who doesn't weigh at all is unlikely to be able to take any appropriate action.
(Ian J. Seath)

Weighing the pig

Evaluation includes a number of things: marking, mock exams, reports, Assessment for Learning (AFL), testing of all kinds, but is always about seeing how effectively students are learning, and then adjusting your teaching so that you can remedy it if they are not making fast enough headway towards their goals. If you can't tell if a student is making progress, then you can't judge what to do next: you can't differentiate accurately, and you can't set targets properly.

Although evaluation has always been important in teaching, the new OFSTED criteria have pushed it into the number one position as far as teaching and learning are concerned. OFSTED has worked out (somewhat belatedly) that you can quite easily tell the difference between an excellent teacher on a bad day and a rubbish teacher on a good one, even in a 20-minute observation, by looking at how their students do relative to other teachers. If in a school, students are making progress, the school is good; if they are not, it is probably not so good. Likewise in the individual class. Where students are making progress, the teacher is good; if they are not, probably not so good. This is, of course, a massive generalisation, and moreover difficult to decide on in the 20 minutes of an observation, with the result that looking at marking and data has become more important in inspections than formerly.

Use the following strategies to build evaluation into your teaching rather than making it an add-on.

Formative and summative assessment

Formative assessment is assessment that is designed to help your students improve their work, while summative assessment simply judges the stage that they have got to. Much anguish is created and time wasted because teachers, students, and parents confuse the two.

Formative assessment, as the name implies, 'forms' a subsequent result so that it is an improvement. It is therefore typically comment-based, takes place during a teaching unit, and will set targets for future improvement at the end of the unit or module. Summative assessment 'sums up' performance, and so will simply give a grade or level of achievement. It typically takes place at the end of the module or unit. Spelling corrections are a simple example of both assessments. If I correct your spellings, asking you to write the wrong ones out again three times, for instance, or show you how to look them up, or teach you spelling rules, then that is formative assessment; if I simply give you a mark out of ten for your spelling test, that is summative.

> ## GET WEAVING
>
> *Students learn best from comments, next best from comments and grades, and worst from grades alone.*

Data is driven by summative assessment, but learning is driven by formative, and so too much attention paid to grades can actually reduce a student's ability to learn and pay attention to the formative feedback. However, combining both kinds of assessment, so that students get a grade and a comment, which might seem to be the happy medium, is often less effective than comments alone. Research (and experience) shows fairly convincingly that students given both grades and comments will ignore the latter in favour of the former. Ideally, you would only ever give students formative assessment and not tell them the grade they are heading for—just the objectives for the next stage—but in practice this is rarely feasible.

Strategies for formative assessment

In good lessons, teachers evaluate all the time—just as footballers evaluate where there is a space to kick the ball—they can tell by a multitude of signs how students are learning and how they could perhaps learn better. So evaluating might just mean making your methods more explicit to the observer, to the student, to the parent, or turning what you do anyway into something that can be data-crunched. It will also mean making the students aware of evaluation so that it becomes formative rather than simply summative, using the principles of Assessment for Learning (AFL). Formative assessment can take place in or out of class.

In-class assessment

Use a learning continuum

A learning continuum lists the stages through which a student must travel in order to achieve the learning objective (see Chapter 2), and will help you with planning as well as with differentiation. Making a learning continuum part of your lesson will help your students understand the stages of learning that they need to get through in order to achieve their goal, and a shared learning continuum is a useful way to check how confident students feel about the stage at which they are. If you are using a PowerPoint, you can repeat the learning continuum slide at regular intervals to check how students rate their progress towards their goals.

Traffic-lighting

This strategy, sometimes called RAG rating, simply means asking students to rate a topic either:

Red (I don't know this.)
Amber (I understand something but am not confident.)
Green (I am confident about this.)

It is a good, quick way of checking where students are with regard to a topic. You can use RAG rating in various ways. The simplest is to get students to highlight topics in their work prior to revision to clarify where they feel most and least confident (due to highlighter limitations this generally turns out to be pink, orange, and green). Similarly, you can relate it to the learning objective at the start of the lesson, and quickly adjust your planning for those students who decide that they already know what you were confidently planning to use as extension work.

Other ways of using this include having red, amber and green cards pinned together with a paperfastener or treasury tag. You can ask students to leave these on their desks, turned to the colour that indicates how they feel they are managing with a task, and this lets you quickly go to those showing red to help them out. Some schools go so far as to have red, orange, and green pages on student planners, so that students can use these as RAG signals in class, by leaving the planner open on the relevant page to indicate if they are struggling with a topic or not.

Emoticons 👆👇 ☺ ☺ ☹

These work in much the same way as RAG rating except you ask students to draw a smiley face ☺, a straight-line face ☺, or a frowning face ☹ to indicate how they feel about a topic or task. You can get really sophisticated here, and also get them to draw other expressions, such as worried or shocked or uncertain. Easier on the highlighter budget, and students like the system. I've similarly tried using thumbs up and down, like Facebook 'likes', but most students find these harder to draw. Also, they are useless for printing on double-sided cards as an indication if a student is struggling, as it's hard to differentiate which way up they are.

Using post-it notes

Post-its are wonderful and endlessly adaptable as a means of assessing. Asking students to note down their ideas or opinions on a post-it at the start of the class, and getting them to put it on a word wall or whiteboard before you start teaching allows you (and any observer) to quickly see where the class is at, and then immediately differentiate accordingly. You can even feed back and divide the post-its into groups, explaining how certain people agree with each other, and then use this as a way of grouping students for independent work later on.

Post-its can be anonymous—which is very good for those students who are nervous about putting forward their ideas, or shy about what they don't understand—and are also low-stakes writing for students who find it hard to commit. I sometimes use different colour post-its for students at different levels, or for different groups, making it easier for me to track answers.

Helping hands ✋

This system uses cards so that students can indicate if they would like to *have* a helping hand or *be* a helping hand (for younger students, you can get them to create the cards for themselves by drawing round their own hands onto card). If the card is coloured differently on both sides (red for needs help, green for can give it), this makes the signal clearer.

This system is especially good for helping students be independent. They can take great pleasure in starting off a topic needing a hand,

and finishing it being able to offer help to others. The two-sided card reduces the likelihood of them becoming completely passive, and can also help teachers to reinforce the 'three before me' style of independence—where you encourage students to refer to 'board', 'book' or 'buddy' before asking you—the 'boss'. If you have a group where all the students on a particular table always need help, you can either sit them with a TA or, better still, split them up so that they can see independence modelled by other students.

Tiered challenges

The 'must, should, could' challenges that are often part of differentiation can also be used to help evaluate student progress during a lesson. Asking students if they feel that they are 'skilled' (using one set of criteria) or 'advanced' (using the next up) is generally more helpful than tying the criteria to grades, which can depress aspiration.

Some schools use the beguiling idea of a 'mild, hot or spicy challenge' when task setting, and again this can be used or adapted easily to evaluate where students are with their understanding. Other ideas include using the image of running or other sports to suggest endurance or speed. Make sure that the language you use encourages aspiration and doesn't make it appear too challenging or intimidating. Inviting students to be springboard or high divers is engaging; suggesting they become shark-pool swimmers might just take the fun out of learning.

Peer and self-assessment

Within a lesson, frequent peer and self-assessment helps you to check that students understand what they are doing, and also helps you to assess how far they are on task and making progress.

In order to effectively peer- or self-assess, you will have to ensure that students understand the assessment criteria for the task that they are attempting, and that they go back over their own work before anyone else tries to mark it. Students well trained in assessment are not only more alert to the processes of their own learning, but can also save you hours of time marking, because they will start to mark for themselves, and revise for themselves, leaving you to do the higher-level marking that is both more interesting and more helpful for them in the long run.

Self-assessment strategies

Mark time with homework

Teach all your students the mantra that it is not worth them handing in to you anything that they can sort out for themselves. Realistically, it is a waste of time you marking errors which students can self-correct—you will be spending time when you could be working out challenging targets for them, correcting capital letters and full stops. Therefore, make sure that students have time to look through their work before they hand it in. If you have set homework, allow five or ten minutes for students to read it through carefully to allow them to spot mistakes before you take it in. This can save a lot of frustration later on.

Make learning objectives clear

In order for students to be able to assess their own progress, they have to be absolutely clear about the learning objective. Make sure that they write it down, or that they have it in their books, that it is on display in the classroom, and that they have discussed how they can evidence achieving it. Using a quiz to elicit the learning objective, giving them the words to assemble into the objective, concealing the objective in part or asking students to predict it, are all ways of ensuring that they don't just mechanically note it down, but also think about it. The simple question: 'How will I be able to tell that you know this?' can be useful in making students think about possible outcomes and evidence.

Be a Tiger Teacher

Like Amy Chua's Tiger Mother, don't accept less than your students' best work. If you have already corrected a child in a point and after self-review they hand in a piece where you come across the mistake again, then hand the piece back and say you will only mark it when they have reviewed it correctly, and that the correction can already be found in their book. This generally encourages students to look more carefully for their mistakes, and to look more carefully at your marking.

Use literacy mats

Literacy mats are useful for both self- and peer-evaluation. They are simply mats, generally laminated, double-sided A3 sheets, which have on them a selection of common subject and literacy errors. Most subject mats have subject-specific ideas on one side, and whole-school literacy on the other, though you can also have double-sided subject-specific ones. It is easy to find ready-made literacy mats on the web, but it can also be helpful to share ideas with neighbouring schools, getting them to create one for one subject area while you offer another. A good (free!) selection of those we created through Oxford City Learning in this way can be found at the resource library at http://oxfordcitylearning.org.uk.

Green penning

A useful strategy for helping students self-assess is to get them to use a particular colour of ink to revise their work. Green pen is popular in many schools which have a 'green pen policy' requiring students to go carefully through their work and check it for specific corrections (especially literacy errors) before they hand it in. Students can also use green pen to respond to marking comments, increasing the sense that the colour marks self-reflection and indicates that they are taking responsibility for their own work.

Highlighter marking

This can be used for both peer- and self-marking, and is especially helpful for visual learners right up to KS5. Where you have more than one set of criteria for assessment, get students to go through their work with one colour of highlighter finding evidence which shows how the first criterion has been fulfilled. Then they can swap highlighter colours with a partner and check for the second, and so on. This then provides an immediate sense of which parts of their response are most useful, and which need to be developed.

Peer-assessment strategies

Train students in marking practice

Allowing students to mark each other's work requires proper training—especially if you are going to escape their complaints about the work not being marked by you. In order to establish peer marking you have to ensure that certain rules are followed, and give some time to establishing this.

You can't simply expect students to know how to mark 'cold'—you have to demonstrate good practice to them, model it, and let them practise on other, less vulnerable work before you let them loose on their classmates. Use whole-class examples and talk through how you mark them before you let students mark each other's work—then they will all be clear about your expectations.

Establish marking routines

Whenever students peer mark, make sure that they use easily recognised formulae, for instance, the 'two stars and a target' rule (that is, two positive things said about the work, and one target for improvement), or WWW and EBI (What Went Well and Even Better If). Let students know the number of elements of the work they are expected to mark. Are they supposed to pick out spelling errors, for instance, and if so, are they expected to offer a correction?

Also, set up 'good behaviour' rules for marking. Curiously, it is not usually a problem that students are too critical—they are likely, on the contrary, to be over-generous in their comments, writing 'well done!' or 'great work' on work that is patently neither well done nor great. Ban the use of emoticons and exclamation marks (and do so in your own marking). To start with, you can even give students a possible comment bank to help them formulate their own ideas.

Tie peer marking to assessment criteria

Never allow students to mark work without setting out what they should be looking for. Firmly establish the criteria for peer marking, as for any marking. Make sure that students understand the criteria for success in a given task, and mark only for that.

To start with, you may like to set fairly mechanical marking tasks, for instance checking if they have used a certain number of key words; as they become more confident, you can set more detailed pieces of marking.

Moderation marking

Moderation is always an interesting and challenging exercise for teachers; let students share in this. Letting students mark with examiner criteria individually, and then letting each table justify a shared mark among themselves, you can then collate all the marks until the room agrees on a mark—by then they should barely need you to justify the mark arrived at, if they have stuck closely to the criteria throughout. It is helpful here to really press students during feedback as to how they have arrived at this mark. Make sure each mark is evidenced.

Mark the marking

Never assume that using self or peer marking means that you don't have to check or look over the work as well. Especially in the early stages of peer marking, it makes sense to go over the marking students have done and check it. The last thing you want in someone's work is an error corrected when it is actually right in the first place, or a misguided offer of 'accurate' spelling which you don't pick up.

Tri-colour marking

If you are checking students' own marking, it can become confusing if you are all using the same colour. It is difficult for the students (or anyone looking at their books) to see where the final authority lies with a comment. Tri-colour marking can really help with this. If you doubt it, imagine the horror of someone thinking a bit of peer marking is actually yours when it is not accurate—as once happened to a colleague of mine.

All tri-colour marking means is that you insist that students write in black ink, and then use colours to distinguish between self-marking (green pen), peer marking (red pen) and teacher marking (purple or blue pen). If you do this then you can tell at a glance whose marking is whose. The student can accept that the teacher's comment is likely to be definitive, and you can readily tell the patterns of self, peer and teacher marking as a department. An added bonus is that giving out the green/red pens is a clear moment of demarcation in a lesson, which alerts students to the task ahead.

Setting SMART targets

If students are setting targets for themselves and others, they will have to be taught carefully how to target-set. It is fatally easy for students to set themselves targets that are too vague to be useful or too ambitious to be achievable. Train students in the language of SMART targets. This acronym dictates that a target should be:

Specific
Measurable
Achievable
Relevant
Time-related

Help students out by giving them specific examples of SMART and non-SMART targets for your subject area, as in the examples below:

Table 6 The difference between vague and SMART targets.

Vague target	SMART target
Improve spellings	Learn three spellings from the list below and be able to use them confidently by this time next week.
Improve vocabulary	Memorise one new vocabulary term to do with holidays each day this week, and use them in a sentence by next Friday's lesson.
Practise times tables	Practise the nine times table for a test next Wednesday in which you should score over 80%.
Use more facts in your essays	Research five key events and their dates which you could have included to improve this essay, and write them in the space below. Indicate with numbers where they should go in the essay.

Plenaries

Plenary sessions, where you sum up learning so far, are essential to evaluate learning. Don't feel that a plenary always has to be at the end of a lesson—in a good lesson, you might have several mini-plenaries throughout, assessing how students have progressed towards the learning objective.

It is really important to ensure that the plenary at the end of a lesson is given sufficient time. Once in a while a quick plenary is fine—especially if you have been evaluating learning throughout—but in general students should expect to return to the purpose of their lesson at the end, and should also expect to be able to articulate their learning. Plenary cards are useful for this (see Chapter 2), and so is targeted and specific questioning.

Mini-plenaries

Mini-plenaries, as the term indicates, are short plenaries that are inserted throughout a lesson to evaluate learning at each stage. If, for instance, you are using a learning continuum, you might have a mini-plenary after each stage to check that your students have fully understood what they need to know before moving on. If they do not understand, you can then adapt the class accordingly.

Unplanned plenaries

Good teachers don't just have plenaries when they have planned them—they are constantly on the alert to how students are getting on, and if they find that a number of them are struggling with a concept that they have already taught, they will be unafraid to stop the class, or create a small group, and have a mini-plenary to test knowledge before letting them go ahead.

Stopping the class like this is not a sign of failure—it is the sign of a confident teacher who is assessing accurately. Make sure that you are aware of the possibility you may have to do this, and build it into your planning. It may be you need a mini-plenary for a certain group only—again, build it into your planning for differentiation.

Failure to launch

Similarly, if you lead a plenary and find out that your students haven't learned what you planned, don't despair and assume that the lesson is a failure. Like an experiment with negative results, it has shown you something valuable—perhaps you need to spend more time on this idea, or the way you planned to teach it wasn't quite right for the group or time of day. Whatever the problem, a plenary will help you sort it, and will moreover allow you to confirm to the students what they have learned—even if what they have learned is how they need to revise that topic. Never be afraid to assert in the plenary that you will have to reframe the next lesson—that is still progress.

Plenary swaps

If possible, try a plenary swap to see if your students have really learned what you planned. In this, you simply arrange with a teacher from another class (works even better with teachers from other subjects) to swap lessons with you for the last ten minutes of a class. Then you have to find out what their students have learned and they have to find out about yours. This really focuses you on making sure that your students have understood their learning well enough to explain it to someone else. It also allows students to teach—which embeds learning even further—and delights students who discover that their English teacher knows nothing about differential calculus.

Making marking manageable

Marking is one of the toughest elements of teaching. The time given for it in planning, preparation, and assessment (PPA) time is ludicrously inadequate, which means that every teacher is inevitably doing hours of overtime just to mark a set of books for each class—or else drowning in a sea of expectation that can lead to marking not getting done at all. It is important to ensure that you keep on top of marking so that you can give regular feedback to your classes, and evaluate their progress effectively.

Make it fast

Mark work as soon as possible after it is handed in. It will be easier when you are still thinking about the ideas that the students are working on. Regular marking that gives rapid feedback is more valuable than detailed marking which only comes once a term. Remember Phil Beadle's wise words—if you don't mark students' work, it is as though, from their point of view, they haven't written it. Even quick 'acknowledgement' marking can be a good thing in these circumstances. Marking quickly and regularly also means that it is less of a chore because there is less to catch up on each time.

There is little point in setting work testing the same set of skills until students have received feedback from the first. Otherwise you will not give students a chance to improve and there is no way that they will be able to show progress. Bear this in mind, and you won't have to mark the same mistakes twice.

Space out your marking

Try NOT to set all your groups a long written task at the same time. If you space out homework tasks so that students are doing a research task, or preparation for an in-class quiz, or a reading task which you will assess in class as well as written tasks then this will automatically lessen the amount of marking you have to do. Making sure you rotate these across classes will further improve your evenings.

Follow school policy

Your school will almost certainly have a marking policy; your department certainly should. Find out what it is, and stick to it. If it seems unmanageable, then don't suffer in silence, but talk to your line manager and work out how to adapt either the policy or your practice. It may well be that it is the policy which needs to change. DON'T be satisfied with the 'old hand' who tells you that no one ever keeps to the policy. It is there for parents and others to find—if it's not right, then make sure it changes to reflect manageable practice.

Work out what's manageable

If you try and mark every child's book every time you teach them, you will probably be exhausted in short order. Instead of trying to do a whole class set in one go, take a few books home every night. Ten books is plenty to mark in one sitting.

GET WEAVING

Use stamps or stickers to save time in marking if you simply want to acknowledge that a task has been done.

Let students know your schedule for marking. If they know that you are planning to mark their books over a weekend, not only are they more likely to complete work by then, but they are also less likely to nag you about completing it instantly.

Time your marking

If you find that a few books are taking you a long time to mark, then set yourself a limited amount of time to complete a set of books, or to complete a given book. You can use a stopwatch or an egg-timer. Ruthless, but this does mean that you get through a lot of books quickly, and it trains you to focus on the essentials. Generally, the more time you spend marking a given task, the faster it gets, so bear this in mind: give yourself leeway on the first few, and then expect to speed up.

Swap marking

Try swapping your marking with another teacher in your department occasionally. It can be easier to mark work when you don't know the student; it is good moderation practice, and it will stop you agonising about that child where you think you know what they meant but they haven't said it. You will also be far more likely to prioritise it if you have a colleague expecting the work back.

Mark for the learning objective

Make sure you mark by looking at the learning objective, and focus only on what the child has or has not achieved in this respect. Be ruthless about not doing more. If you use the wording of the learning objective you will also speed up your marking because you will not have to be thinking of new things to say.

Summative assessment: Who is assessment for?

One of the problems with evaluating students' work is that we evaluate it for different purposes at different times. Be honest with yourself about whom the evaluation is for, and adapt what you do accordingly.

Reporting to students

Share your ideas

Assessment should be a two-way process. It is not all about whether you can tell if students are learning—it should also be about whether they feel that they are. For evaluation to be useful, students need to become more reflective about their own progress, and less reliant upon you to measure it for them. Good AFL practice should mean that students are aware of the assessment criteria that you are using, and understand how they are going to be assessed. They should become able to judge themselves and others, and in doing so will become more independent learners.

It's not about you

The pressure on schools to show that they have achieved a particular percentage of A*—C grades, or that students have achieved a certain rate of progress from Key Stage 2 can mean that students—always quick to pick up on adult concerns—can start to feel that you are more invested in their educational progress than they are. And this is a very bad idea. The moment that little Lucy feels that she is doing you a personal favour by completing her homework, darkness falls on the world and there will be weeping and gnashing of teeth.

I remember once listening to a teacher talking to a boy who had misbehaved during exam preparation. The teacher was earnestly trying to explain how important it was for this child to get his GCSEs, but the boy concerned was affecting lack of interest, maintaining that the whole notion of exam practice was inherently boring, but that he would be fine on the day itself. Finally, the teacher said: 'You know that we are held accountable if you don't get your grade....', and just like that, the boy's interest was lost. You could see the little flicker in his eyes that indicated that his expectations had been met, and he switched off. Yes, his expression said, I knew that you were really in it for yourself, not for me.

Don't do this. Don't let students think that evaluation of whatever kind is for us, not for them. Or if you do, then don't make it their problem if they fail. I have actually had some success by telling students that I am testing them just for my own records, and please don't make any special effort, as I won't tell them how they have done—it's just for my own information. They instantly become desperate to find out how to improve.

Reporting to school

The one thing that summative assessment is useful for is to track students accurately. Because of this, it is of the utmost importance that you are honest about your data. Think about why you are giving it, and be as accurate as possible. If your school is not completely clear about—for instance—the difference between a 'working at' grade and a predicted grade, then ask them to clarify. You certainly won't be the only member of staff grateful for the information, and unless everyone is working on the same information it will be worse than useless to collate it.

Make sure that whenever you give a grade that will be used for data entry, that you can justify it with evidence that you can easily retrieve. Make sure that your marking is cross-checked and moderated by someone else at regular intervals (this should be automatic within a good department—if not, institute it) and occasionally ask a friend's advice if you are not sure about a grade. There is more advice from boards than ever before about judging exam grades—use it.

Reporting to parents

Reporting to parents is an important part of evaluation—and will sometimes be the part which the student will value most highly. In more leisured days, teachers would wittily, pithily or inaccurately sum up their students (sometimes being appallingly rude) in the kind of statements that are immortalised in school reports of the rich and famous, where Margaret Thatcher is noted as being 'ambitious' or Churchill as a 'troublemaker', with Einstein likely 'not to amount to anything'. Now data has often taken the place of the leisured handwritten comment, with comments (if they appear at all) often generated from target banks, and all tending to focus definitively on the assessment criteria and not on the student's personality or attitude to learning, itself generally summed up by a number instead of a cutting piece of wit.

Because of the prevalence of data-driven reporting, parents' evenings often become more important as ways of conveying your evaluations to parents. If your assessment of a child's progress is aimed at parents, consider what they would like or need to know about their child's development in your subject, and in their attitude to learning. Record the things that the student does well; explain what the child has covered in class; if you use grades or levels, explain what they mean in relation to an average or an age-related score. Give parents examples of the kind of problems or questions that their child has learned to answer.

When you ask students about their learning, or ask them which part of a lesson they have enjoyed, keep a record and save it for parents' evening. Even a brief note in your planner or register will be helpful when it comes to parents' evening, or report-writing, and allows you to give that sense of personalised learning which is so important. Note if a child has particularly enjoyed a discussion, or a problem; notice also if a topic makes the child nervous or anxious.

Have an idea of what you expect the parents to do about their child's learning. With any kind of evaluation, it is important that you give a sense of 'what next'? In other words, what is the point of sharing this information with this person? For parents, in particular, it is really helpful to be given direct ideas as to what they can do to help their child's learning. If they have come to parents' evening, they are, after all, committed to the extent that they have given up their time to find out how their child is doing. Encourage them for that, praise them for their concern, and then explain what else they could do to help. Some schools or departments provide general or subject-specific revision booklets with helpful hints. Equally helpful can be a set of mail-merged cards to hand out, with apparently individualised advice.

How can you tell if students are learning?

Problems tend to occur with assessment because students are unhappy with summative grades. It is not enough for them to know that they have got a C; they want to know how they can make it into a B. What went wrong? How did they miss it? Can they persuade you to change your mind? As a result, it is often helpful to divide up summative and formative assessment really clearly for students. You can use an analogy like that of a race, with the weeks of a unit as miles of the race. Their final result will show how fast they ran, how hard they tried—but you will not coach them when they achieve it, but while they're on the way; you can only help them learn from their result in readiness for the next race.

Of course you want to know how your students are getting on; of course you want to find out how they are learning. Nonetheless, the more that you poke and prod them in assessment terms, the more likely they are to switch off, decide that they have had quite enough of all this learning, thank you very much, and go back to staring creatively out of the window. Like plants growing, students need to be allowed to learn without being disturbed by grading too much. Try and lift them up to see how well they are doing, and you will have broken roots, and wilting plants. No matter which metaphor you choose, too much assessment can be problematic.

6

Record and Reflect: Embedding Learning

Not choice but habit rules the unreflective herd.
(William Wordsworth)

Just as one spoils the stomach by overfeeding and thereby impairs the whole body, so can one overload and choke the mind by giving it too much nourishment. For the more one reads the fewer are the traces left of what one has read; the mind is like a tablet that has been written over and over. Hence it is impossible to reflect; and it is only by reflection that one can assimilate what one has read. If one reads straight ahead without pondering over it later, what has been read does not take root, but is for the most part lost.
(Arthur Schopenhauer)

What did you do at school today?

Recording learning is one of the most important things that you need to do as a teacher—and one of the easiest to forget if you are trying to teach an engaging lesson. Sometimes, because what is going on in the classroom is good, because students are excited and enthusiastic, it is easy to forget to record what they have done. Weeks later, looking through their books, what evidence will you, they, or anyone else see of what they have learned? Recording learning in concrete form is the underpinning of an excellent lesson.

The biggest reason for doing this is so that students themselves remember. Most teachers, I am sure, remember the process of taking notes in a lecture or seminar, notes that perhaps you never really read through again. Finding them later on, even years later, you can recall the lecture even if all you did was doodle. The recording process itself helps to pin the ideas into your mind. In the same way, if students record what they have learned, and more importantly *reflect* on what they have learned, the learning 'sticks' much more powerfully than if they just breeze out of the door and onto the next lesson. Plenary questions can help—so can asking them to write a note to their parents explaining what they have just learned—they may even then employ it in answer to the perennial parental question about what they did at school.

Starting writing: fear of flying

Fear of writing is like fear of flying. Students who are nervous will delay and delay so as not to get to the departure gate, often requiring immense amounts of teacher time to drag out a sentence or two. The sad truth is that you cannot force a child to write—any more than you can force them to do anything; you can only persuade, engage, and charm. Putting pressure on nervous students will tend to make them dig their heels in—like toddlers, they will stall you and become confrontational rather than head in the direction you would like.

One reason why students dislike writing is that they are afraid of failure. In order to avoid this, they will not start. Sometimes it can be as simple as shame about handwriting, or worries about their spelling. Students who can be confident and articulate in class will at times manifest with behavioural problems when asked to put down their ideas in written form for these reasons. To cure this problem—as with fear of flying—give control back to the student. Make recording ideas an unthreatening or fun task where the writing seems to be the least prominent element. There are a variety of ways in which you can do this:

Comfort is king

There's not much you can do about plastic chairs, but within reason, try and make sure that students are comfortable when they are writing. For instance, it can be genuinely distracting for a left-handed student to be seated to the right of a right-handed one—their elbows will keep clashing. Make sure you remember to seat left-handers to the left of a two-seater table so that they can write without interference. Have spare biros on hand for those who will claim that their biro ran out, and offer them with a smile. Make students feel that you are there to help, not to tyrannise.

Similarly, try and make sure you are not asking students to write when they have to turn around or sit awkwardly to see the board; if you are asking them to write without desks to lean on, give them clipboards or something to lean on. It is amazing how something as small as a couple of sheets of paper to put under a worksheet will make the difference between defiance and compliance.

Low-stakes writing

Like a shop with a special offer at the door that lures in buyers to open their purse, the canny teacher will get a student writing in some low-stakes way at the start of the lesson. Post-it notes, whiteboards, and small slips of paper are useful for this. The point about this kind of writing is that it is unthreatening. Anxiety about producing writing is lessened when no one will seemingly be assessing it.

A post-it starter, apparently anonymous, can be an easy way to quickly assess writing confidence. In the same way, mini whiteboards which can be used for suggestions or answers that students hold up to the teacher or share with partners, can then be rapidly adjusted or erased if the student is unhappy with what has been written.

Throwaway writing

As with low-stakes writing, this is unthreatening—and also harnesses the natural desire of a student to 'chuck' bits of paper across a room. Get students to write answers or suggestions on scraps of paper, then get them to screw them up and throw them to another student or another group, who will then add to the idea/correct the answer and either throw it back or pass it on.

GET WEAVING

Let students turn the paper bits into mini paper aeroplanes for maximum enjoyment—add names and they can get a prize for the most aerodynamic creations.

As a sophistication of this strategy, you can colour-code scraps of paper so that you can identify which group they came from, and make every member of the group responsible for what is written on their group's colour.

Beautiful writing

For the student who is self-conscious about their writing, try offering them a choice of pens and paper to make writing more special. Ask a student to create a beautiful label for a display, for instance, where the focus is on the style of writing and not its length, or get them to try out a quill pen and write a letter to be tea-stained and scorched about the edges, so that it looks ancient. Allow them to try writing in felt-tip, or teach them how to do headlines in bubble writing or imitate different fonts. Many students who have not had a great deal of training in handwriting become fascinated by these kinds of strategies which slow down the writing process, and will then happily practise handwriting for homework.

Postman Pat delivers

With this strategy, students write on small pieces of card a response to the learning question at the start of the lesson—or simply write what they know about the topic. The response can happily be 'I don't know' or 'nothing' at this stage, which generally draws in the reluctant writers.

At intervals throughout the lesson, a mini-plenary happens, where one student becomes 'Postman Pat' and delivers one of the cards back to each student (this can be their own or someone else's). The student has to read the 'letter', reflect on the answer, and write a more developed answer.

GET WEAVING

Try creating postcard templates for your pieces of card to make this strategy more convincing.

Even if they start off with 'I still don't know anything', generally students will—simply through the teaching and through reading a variety of possible responses—have written a more developed opinion by the end of the lesson.

Flipbooks

This seems to work especially well for history, or any subject where a narrative order of events is important. A flipbook is one of those small books which students delight in creating and playing with—where a small character drawn on each page changes infinitesimally each page to create a flickering moving picture effect when the whole is flipped through at speed. Here the lure is that in exchange for writing a little on each page, they get to create a flipbook with character pictures. I've seen this used effectively as a way of recording the order of experiments, with imaginatively drawn explosions on the pictures.

Writing on hands

A twist on a handwriting focus, this allows those students who like to doodle on their hands a way of using them to remember key points for a paragraph or answer. You can either let students write on each finger, with the main point in the palm, or for the neater/more anxious of parental reaction, draw round a hand on a page and use the structure in the same way. For some reason this doesn't seem to count as writing, but it will encourage students to start getting their ideas down in written form.

Magic writing

For this, I use the cheap 'invisible ink' pens you can get in toyshops (one between a group is plenty). Ask a group to work on a problem, and then write down their best solution in invisible ink (they should keep a copy for their table as a record).

The other groups then rotate and try to come up with their solutions, or guess the first group's answer (whichever you prefer), with a final unveiling of the answers in invisible ink at the end. Students are often more confident about writing when they know it cannot be immediately read. Again, good classroom management means that you do need to be aware of who is writing what, to deal with the inevitable results if some students decide to go off-task.

GET WEAVING

For a science lesson, try using lemon juice as invisible ink (the stuff sold in little plastic lemons works fine). Heat the paper gently and the writing should turn brown.

Doodling

While you are talking, or if you want students to take notes, ask them to take notes in picture form, through doodles. You can then swap the doodles and see if students can reconstruct the points through their friends' 'notes'.

Cheating

Again, students enjoy this enormously. The rules are that you give each student a small square of paper. On this they have to put as much information as they possibly can so as to answer a given problem or exam question. Students will often find ingenious ways of making writing tiny, or abbreviating ideas, so as to fit on as much as possible, before starting to answer the question concerned. This gives you the delightful sight of a whole room apparently cheating while actually being on task.

Developing writing

Often teachers complain that some students are so reluctant to write that getting them to take notes or develop ideas in written form is time-consuming and can become a battle. In these circumstances it is not surprising that some teachers lose heart and stop pestering children to write, or get them to do the bare minimum—but this only exacerbates the problem for future years, with the result that students can get to GCSE years without feeling relaxed and confident about writing.

Part of getting students to feel comfortable about writing is to build it into part of their normal lesson routine, which is one reason why recording learning should be a part of every lesson. Left to themselves, students who are uncomfortable about writing will not develop this skill outside school, and need careful handling from teachers right across the curriculum to build their confidence. If they know that in every lesson they will be doing some writing it quickly becomes less of a chore.

Developing extended writing is immensely important for some subjects, and it is not something that should be neglected in any—even maths teachers are finding that students are now getting points for accuracy of explanation. More important than exam requirements, developing students through writing encourages independence and gets them to think carefully about what they are saying.

Writing frames

Writing frames went through a period of being immensely popular; they are still used in some schools, but far less, probably because they became unnecessarily restrictive. Used creatively, writing frames can be a way of encouraging students to write independently, and will transition smoothly into independent writing.

A good writing frame will imitate the process of argument or discovery or explanation through clear chronological or other signposts. Often simply giving students a choice of these will be enough to start them off on a sentence: 'Firstly', 'At the start of this experiment', 'Initially', 'In the beginning', 'In 1910', 'In Chapter 1' can all be used as clear but simple scaffolding signals for a writing frame.

Subsequent paragraphs should be scaffolded in the same way, perhaps with a brief prompt that indicates the expected length or direction of an answer. Using a table for a writing frame can be helpful in that it gives an indication of the length expected for each section, and again this kind of structuring can make writing seem less formidable for students.

Try getting students, in discussion, to create their own writing frames. As part of a planning activity, ask them what should go at the start of each section of writing, what should be included in each paragraph and so on, and then get them to follow their own—or a partner's—instructions.

Slow writing

Slow writing is an excellent way of developing writing where students are insecure, because it restricts the amount of writing that they have to do, and gives them a clear scaffolding for independent writing. With slow writing, students are given a direct instruction about the form or content of each sentence they write. A website by Triptico http://www.triptico.co.uk/media/temp/slowWriting.html will even provide you with online slow writing instructions six sentences at a time (such as 'sentence one must start with an embedded subordinate clause'). The instructions will update and change each time you use it—terrific for computer-based lessons.

Slow writing is especially good for creative writing, where you could ask students to start a sentence with an adverb, include a semicolon, or write a sentence exactly twelve words long, or get them to choose instructions out of a hat, or create instructions that they then swap with each other. However, it should be by no means limited to English lessons. The strategy can also be useful for other subjects, as long as you remember that you can replace direct grammatical instructions with other kinds of instruction to do with the task, for instance including a particular key word in a sentence, or adding in a cause or a date.

Speed paragraphs

Many teachers favour PEE (Point, Example, Explanation) or PEEL paragraphs (PEE + Link), which are not only a bit tired, but rather limiting for students. The problem with your classic PEE paragraph is that it doesn't help students to develop analysis. Indeed the danger is that they are likely to end up being circular: 'In *Of Mice and Men* Lennie likes stroking soft things. He says "I like to stroke soft things" which shows that he likes to stroke soft things'. To avoid this, try the acronym SPEED:

> **S** is for **Signpost**—this indicates where in the text you are, or narrows in on a particular issue.
> **P** is for **Point**—this is your clear answer to the question.
> **E** is for **Example**—showing your evidence.
> **E** is for **Explanation**—which explains what you understand by the evidence.
> **D** is for **Discussion or Development**—where you add to or show a different perspective on your explanation.

For example, in an English SPEED paragraph you might get the following:

> **S** In chapter 12 of *Lord of the Flies*
> **P** Ralph shows the qualities of a true leader.
> **E** When the officer asks 'Who's boss here?', he immediately responds 'I am', even though Jack has taken the leadership from him.
> **E** Ralph's lack of hesitation, combined with the adverb 'loudly' suggests that he is confident enough to assert his leadership, now that the adults have returned, and implies that he is brave enough to take responsibility for what has happened.
> **D** However, the fact that Jack thinks of coming forward, but changes his mind suggests not only that he is not prepared to take responsibility, but also that he is quick-witted and can see that whoever leads might now be blamed for the deaths of Piggy and Simon.

The good thing about SPEED is not only do you avoid the jokes about students PEEing all over the place, but you get a more developed piece of writing, because it forces them to give more space and time to the development of ideas than to the initial thought. The use of the signpost stops students confusing a signpost with a point, and again inclines them to make a clearer point. The method can be used for all subjects across the curriculum, but has been shown to be especially effective in English, science, humanities subjects, and DT.

Consequences

Consequences, like the parlour game of the same name, relies on students each writing a section of an answer. Unlike traditional consequences, it relies on them reading what their partners have written. The peer pressure of others writing spurs on even those less inclined to develop their own work, and at worst allows students to see models of writing from their peers.

GET WEAVING

For a faster version of 'Consequences', get students to write only a sentence, or even only a word before passing on the paper.

One of the most effective ways of doing this is to start with an exam question, get students to write the first paragraph of a response in a given time, then get them to pass it on. The second person has to read the first paragraph and continue the argument, adjusting their ideas as may be necessary. Each turn needs slightly longer as the students have to read through and think about the previous pieces of writing.

Storyboarding

Storyboarding is a popular strategy, which can also be used to help encourage writing. To storyboard a narrative, a series of events, a timeline, a process or an experiment, is fairly straightforward. To start with, ask students merely to produce pictures with simple captions.

Always demonstrate through stick or easily-imitated cartoon figures so as to reassure those who are not confident about their own artistic talents that you do not need them to draw perfectly.

Once students are happy to do this, ask them to add in more detail; for instance, you might go from a one-line to a three-line caption; you might create more sections of the story so they have to write more; you might ask them to add in speech bubbles and dialogue. All these strategies increase the amount of writing produced, and build writing confidence. Finally, you can ask them to transfer the storyboard into written form, using each panel as a scaffold or paragraph start, and describing the pictures as a way into adding depth.

Word-limit writing

Paradoxically, limiting the number of words that you permit students to use for a task is a good way to get them wanting to write more. 'Mini sagas' for instance are stories of exactly 50 words which invariably mean that students write more and have to edit them down—excellent for confidence and for editing skills.

You can use the same strategy of limiting the amount written as good practice for short-answer questions in exams. Tell students that they have to express an idea in exactly 20 words, and they start to think carefully about what is essential. Similarly, you can get students to précis an article or another student's answer to a given word-limit. To précis an article into a given compass is an excellent reading exercise and also a good way of ensuring that reading homework is done, and the work thoroughly understood.

Creative writing

Students who often enjoy storytelling at key stage 2 or key stage 3 can find that they miss it in secondary school. Try allowing students to turn factual accounts into stories or diary entries to encourage longer writing. Writing an account of an event from different perspectives, for history, geography, business, politics, or English, for instance, can be used as an effective display as well.

Quotiebix

I first used this as a way of helping students to remember quotations, but it can be as readily used for formulae, times tables, dates and facts or key words. It is the task that got me the best parental feedback ever from parents' evening. To create quotiebix, you get students (and staff) to bring in old cereal packets. When you have enough for one per person in your group:

- Distribute one box each.

- Go through cereal packet design. Point out how we tend to remember things like the ingredients because we stare unthinkingly at them over the breakfast table.

- Get students to take the boxes carefully apart to reveal the plain cardboard inside.

- On the plain surface, let the students design a personalised cereal-packet-style set of quotations, reminders of key points, facts or whatever else you want them to remember.

- Reassemble the box with double-sided tape so that the newly-decorated surface is on the outside.

- Students take the boxes home, place on the breakfast table, and put the inner packaging of their cereal inside, thus reading the new information over breakfast.

- This works even for students who don't eat cereal—and as parents pointed out to me, encourages them to sit at the table for a little longer.

Showing off writing: display

Display is one of the most important ways of recording what your students have learned in a way which constantly reminds them of it. Display, and an attractive classroom environment in general, is something that OFSTED particularly likes to see, and it is definitely not something that relies on your school's base environment. Some of the shiniest, brightest academies have no-poster policies that result in walls looking bland and dull, whereas otherwise dingy older schools can look amazing with creatively-used display.

GET WEAVING

Displays inside the classroom should focus on things that will help your students remember key ideas and concepts; outside the classroom they should show off student work.

Creating displays in your classroom is one other way in which you can make it your—and your students' territory. If you have any issues with behaviour management, it will help your room be a space which reflects your authority. Use student writing for display work, have a 'working wall' or 'word wall' where post-its or other small pieces of writing will be placed every lesson to get them used to the idea that their writing is an important part of the lesson; seeing their work on display outside will reassure them that it is valuable.

Departmental display

Ideally, when anyone comes into your department, it should be immediately obvious what the area is all about. Large, bright displays should catch the attention of students and staff and make them feel that they are now in the distinctive territory of a particular subject area. If you have whole-school policies or programmes (such as literacy or numeracy displays, or tutorial notices) that need to be up, then make sure that they are individualised for your subject. Key word displays are always useful, and can be made entertaining by the use of cartoons. I particularly like the maths one which has one angle comforting another that it's not at all obtuse, and the science one where a bouncer refuses two double helixes admission to a club with the laconic 'no genes'.

Some basics hold true whatever department you are in. Try to make displays striking, informative and colourful. Keep them maintained and neat, with covers or lamination if possible. Make it someone's job to watch for edging coming away, or any graffiti, and repair flaws immediately. Try using unusual backing paper or 3D elements to add interest. Place your displays carefully—creating a vast 3D one in a busy corridor is just asking for damage, but the same display in a more open space will be respected.

Below are some ideas for instantly appealing displays in individual departments, culled from various schools. You may well find that you can adapt these ideas for your own department, or that they inspire you to revitalise your displays. If you run short of display ideas it is always worth asking another department for advice, because, as with teaching, they will often have a different and useful take on the topic. In any case, try and make sure that your displays include key words, that they are visually appealing, that, if possible, they include some 3D element or unusual materials, and that they are useful.

Maths displays

- Displays about 'maths language', which involve the difference between a table and a table, takeaway and a takeaway, tree and a tree, pi and a pie and so on, well illustrated.

- Displays for 'Pi day' (March 14th) involving many pictures of pies with different measurements worked out, and other pi-related ideas. A display of tries at Buffon's needle, for instance, is effective as an ongoing and active display.

- Shape finders—so, for instance, a collection of pictures about triangles found in the 'real world', ranging from snaps of construction sites or warning road signs to Doritos stuck to the display board. Easy to do for different shapes, and students get very enthusiastic about this.

- Geometrical landscapes—pictures of different landscapes (cityscapes are obvious ones, but the natural world works well, particularly pictures culled from *The Earth from the Air*) with geometrical forms overlaid to show the inherent geometry of landscapes. A useful way to remind students of the etymology and spelling of geometry, literally 'earth-measuring'.

- Matching prices (using pictures of coins or notes in named purses or wallets) to different objects, asking what can a particular celebrity buy.

- Times table displays which explain easy ways to remember tables. For instance an easy way to remember the nine-times table is to put both hands in front of you and mentally number your fingers one to ten. If you want to calculate a multiple of nine, put down the relevant finger, e.g. your third finger for 3x9, and the fingers on the left of it (2) will represent tens, the ones on the right (7) units, giving the correct answer 3x9=27. Photos of this process can really fix it into children's minds, and will often encourage them to try it for themselves. Asking children which times table sum they find hardest and how they remember it can also lead to some entertaining displays.

- Negative number displays using the sea as an image to explain negative numbers—(underwater is negative, above the water positive) numbered fish can be moved up and down to make it interactive, with flying fish and jumping fish showing positive numbers.

- Displays of sports statistics, or calculations about probability that relate (for instance) to the chances of goal scoring in the premier league, or the relative speeds of runners.

- A 'maths is everywhere' display that presents examples of maths from everyday life, e.g. working out the calories in food, deciding on the best value between two special offers, and so on.

- Times tables calculations drawn on windows around the department for a week until EVERYONE knows what 6x8 is.

Science displays

Biology displays

- A 'micromonsters' display of enlarged pictures of insects and other small creatures, with accompanying text labelling key common features. Fake butterflies can make this an engaging 3D display. You can also arrange the micromonsters into a series of Venn diagrams or branches to illustrate similarities and differences visually.

- An interactive leaf display where students bring in different examples of leaves and try to label and identify the different kinds of plant (can start with an outdoor lesson).

- A 'cells' competition—students are asked to make cell models out of a wide variety of materials—results can include plasticine, embroidered and cake versions!

- A series of food webs using string to make the connections. You can add in real items such as bones and plants to enliven this.

- A diagram of the alimentary canal drawn on a classroom floor or corridor. (Try liquid chalk marker pens for this—they last but can easily be wiped away if necessary.)

- An 'ordinary object from an unusual angle' display of close-up pictures of skin or human hair, for instance, which invites students to guess what the pictures represent.

Physics displays

- A 3D or 2D display of transport such as ships, planes, cars (using toys), explaining the forces acting on each when they are in motion.

- A 'sundial' display that uses natural or artificial light to help throw shadows and explain ideas of shadow and light.

- A display about circuits and conductors that uses real wires and connectors to create a 3D effect.

- Display that illustrates different types of movement such as 'push', 'pull', 'jump', 'swing', 'turn' and so on, using everyday examples (this can be a display that children contribute to by bringing in their own examples).

- A 'Theme Park' display, with pictures of rides, explaining which forces are present in each stage of each ride.

- A mobile display of the solar system, hanging from the ceiling. A whole-department twist on this is to assign rooms to different planets and their moons. With some ingenuity you can use the distances between classes to indicate the relative distances between planets, and even name classes after the major planets, theming displays to indicate, for instance, the origin of the names of the classical gods, or the gases in the atmosphere, or the temperatures estimated on each surface.

Chemistry displays

- A display that demonstrates the ways in which fireworks are constructed, and how different chemicals produce different colour effects. Dissected and 'exploded' fireworks make an attractive 3D effect. Students can design their own fireworks for additional interest.

- A display about the chemistry of cooking, demonstrating the different reactions used in cooking and how they work every day (try *Modernist Cuisine: The Art and Science of Cooking* for some ideas).

- A display that illustrates the everyday uses of chemicals (for instance washing up), and 'unnoticed' everyday chemical reactions such as rusting, ideally with student input.

- A display of different dyes created from chemicals illustrating their effects on the same kind of square of white sheeting—a twist on this is getting students to see what dyes they can create from natural substances. This project is interesting in itself, and you can then add the substances (or pictures of them) to the display of dyed material.

- The chemistry of drugs. Fascinating to students (though controversial) and can be readily linked to PSHE.

- A display that demonstrates the chemistry of forensic analysis, perhaps including some student chromatography.

English displays

- An English timeline display that shows when authors were writing, with examples of their most famous works.

- A map of the British Isles that uses stickers and string to show where famous UK authors came from, where they worked, and where they died (sometimes the same place, sometimes an intriguing track to follow).

- A language change display that illustrates how language changes. One way of doing this is to use different versions of the English

Bible, or translations of classical texts from different periods to highlight how the same ideas are expressed differently. Also try comparing newspapers from different eras in language terms, or famous speeches.

● Displays linked to books can be especially useful if they in effect storyboard the book, using images from films or illustrations. A moving display can include the start and finish of a story, and have velcroed units that can be moved around—introduce a few new ones each week to see how students manage to include them (Velcro spot stickers are readily available).

● A display that considers castings for an imagined film of a particular text—pictures of different actors are placed on the board with student ideas as to why they would suit each role noted around them—can end in a class vote.

● A 3D story display relating to a novel (for instance *Wuthering Heights*) that demonstrates the landscape of the novel, and adds in incidents in the relevant place.

● A display of how to analyse a poem, laying out some basic ideas about how to approach an unseen text, with the poem changing each week.

● A brilliant idea from my colleague Sarah Marcus: try having departmental 'shelfies'. This means that each English teacher takes a photo of their home bookshelf (real or can be planned). Students have to try and link up the teacher to the shelfie, the only clues being the books chosen. Easy to adapt for a class of students as a project to encourage aspirational reading.

● Displays of different newspaper accounts of the same news story can be used to highlight the differences in reporting bias and language.

● A display which compares a poem such as 'The Charge of the Light Brigade' with the newspaper report which inspired it, picking out details of language.

● Newspaper poetry—where poems are created by blacking out words in a newspaper report to leave the ones you wish to be read.

- Analysing a series of news images with matching caption or headline is a good way into discussing word play, and can be easily updated.

- Imitation poetry—where students imitate a particular genre, such as the sonnet, or else try to write a modern version of or response to an older poem.

- A reading tree—create a large, bare tree outline or tree trunk, get teachers, students and parents to write the name of a book they love on a paper 'leaf', then organise them into branches and twigs (genres and authors). You can create a tree and have it leafless until people write on a leaf, or change the colour of a leaf when it is written on.

Humanities displays

History displays

- A timeline that runs down the corridor, showing the major events of English and world history. Try tying into other departments and getting them to add in significant moments for their subject in a key colour for each department.

- One school I visited had a whole corridor converted to a WW1 trench. You don't have to go that far, but trying to create a vivid reconstruction, even in a small area of the department, is something that is very appealing to students and draws in other departments to help.

- Local history display—showing maps of the school area, with photos if possible, before the school was built or developed to its present size.

- Family history display—a selection of family trees of famous people, matched by those of students or teachers, to show how our ancestors lived at the time of famous people.

- A reportage display, comparing eyewitness reports of events such as the great Plague or the Great Fire of London with eyewitness reports of 9/11.

- A display which matches historical events to more modern events which connect to them, for instance, Queen Victoria's Jubilee with Queen Elizabeth II's, or the Crimean war with current conflicts in the Crimea.

Geography displays

- A vivid depiction of the water cycle, with cotton-wool clouds and cellophane water, and glittering snowflakes from Christmas-themed table confetti can look spectacular to brighten up a dull corridor.

- A simple map of the world, with stickers or flags indicating where everyone in the school comes from—lovely to pair with citizenship or MFL as well.

- A display running down a corridor wall, of a river and its geography from source to sea. Or a giant hallway/stairwell cross-section of a volcano or a mountain.

- Coastal erosion lends itself well to 3D work, with polystyrene cliffs sticking easily to display boards.

- Rainforest displays—with treetops reaching above the display board onto the wall. Real plants can be incorporated into this display for added effect—palm leaves last for ages, as do shiny leaves such as *Monstera delicosa*, and tiny spider plants can be nurtured in test-tubes embedded in *papier maché* trees.

Politics and business displays

- A large display board can be used to create 'Prime Minister's Question Time'; including a mock-up of the Houses of Parliament. Pictures of politicians with speech-bubble sound bites about topical matters can be added, with the topics changed weekly. Student opinion can be added into speech bubbles or post-its to comment on the topic, and information labels can describe each politician's role, and the party divisions.

- 'Dragon's-Den'-style presentations with different entrepreneurial ideas competing against each other for display attention. For a really useful student entrepreneur project get them to set up a company creating displays for busy teachers!

- A 3D display that illustrates the processes of production of a garment such as a T-shirt, demonstrating the proportion of money given to each person in the stage of production—you need two T-shirts at least, one that can be cut up in pieces to be assigned to each stage.

- An explanation of what it means to be an entrepreneur, with snippets of biographical detail from famous entrepreneurs. These are especially good if chosen to illustrate how failure and risk is a feature of building up a business.

- A 'recruitment and training' display that outlines an imaginary job, and then gives the job description and different candidates— passing students have to vote for which candidate will be successful.

RE, philosophy and citizenship displays

- Displays that illustrate where money donated to a charity goes, literally tracking the journey of the money in your pocket to buy aid.

- A recycling display, showing different materials found in litter around the school, and showing how long it takes them to biodegrade, and how they can be recycled effectively.

- A display of the major world religions, showing what they have in common, as well as their differences.

- Art from the major religions—examples of art or literature associated with the major religions, explaining why it takes the form it does—for instance why Islamic art is often geometrical.

- Quotations from major philosophers and thinkers, perhaps creating a timeline of thought, or a 'big issues' board, with a range of opinions around a central question (such as 'Does God Exist?').

- A two-part display that illustrates the beauty of the world and the harm that people do to it—so, for instance, happy people round a camp fire are paired against a forest fire, or a top-specification fridge is paired against a polar bear on a melting ice floe with comments about the ways they connect. This links to geography, but also emphasises responsibility.

- A litter chart showing which areas of the school have most and least litter over a given time.

PSHE displays
- A 'problem page' display of information about sexual and mental health, with problems in speech bubbles, and answers giving contact details of support services.

- An anti-bullying display with a range of posters created by students.

- A healthy living display which offers choices between different kinds of foods and explains what they contain (can usefully use litter wrappers as illustrations of junk food).

- Displays against smoking or drugs which illustrate health issues. Getting students to design what they would put on cigarette packets as health warnings can be very powerful. Wire wool makes an excellent 3D 'smoker's lung'.

- A 'feelings' display which asks 'How do you feel today?' with illustrations of different facial expressions, then underneath 'How do you look?' This can be good at indicating that people don't always show their feelings outwardly.

- For a classroom or tutor room, an 'acronym poetry' display is attractive. Students have to describe another student by thinking of positive qualities assigned to the initial letters of their name (for instance, Felix might be **F**abulous, **E**nergetic, **L**oving, **I**maginative and an e**X**pert **X**ylophonist).

Art/design displays

Resistant materials displays
- A 3D display that has examples of different materials in everyday use—for example, wood, metal, plastic—all labelled and brought in by students to be stuck on a display board.

- A display showing the details for a project from design to completion, with different designs and reasons for choosing them.

- A bridge or other artefact labelled with all the engineering elements of each component, from the screws and bolts to the tension of wires. Also works well for physics.

- Pictures of items from catalogues, sorted and labelled according to the materials with which they are constructed.

- A display showing different designs for an item with the same basic function (e.g. a table or chair) labelling the differences and reasons for them.

Food technology displays

- A 'larder' display, where a picture of a store cupboard, open to show basic ingredients, has string running from the different ingredients to pictures of the dishes that they can be used to create. Obviously, each ingredient can be used for multiple dishes. This works best when the pictures are of meals created by students.

- Display of the entrants to a 'back of the fridge challenge' or 'Masterchef' competition, where students are challenged to design a recipe to use up a certain list of ingredients, and limited as to what they can add to it. Can be very ingenious!

- Pictures of 'funny face pizza' or cakes designed by students.

- 'The Great (insert name of school) Bake-Off' display—cakes, biscuits, and so on made by students, judged and photographed, with reviews written by the judges.

- A 'fridge' display, showing where different foods should be kept so as to maintain optimum freshness. Plastic bags and polystyrene are good for modelling food that is light enough to stick up on the wall.

Textile displays

- A display that shows a cushion cover, for instance, from start to finish, in several stages, from first design to completed article, with increasingly completed covers along the board at each stage. Above and below the covers, you can stick the extra materials needed at each stage, as for instance dye, buttons, embroidery thread, patches to applique and so on, until you reach the final design.

- Different textile samples brought in by students, grouped according to type or design or colour with illustrative labels.

- A soft toy 'exploded' to show how it is made, with each component labelled (try to have two, so one can be seen intact next to it for the soft-hearted).

- A display showing the processes of tie-dying or batik printing, with step by step examples on real fabric.

Art/graphics displays

- Displays that demonstrate how to achieve each assessment objective (AO) in art or graphics—making evident that it is not all about creating pretty pictures.

- Competitions such as 'artist of the term/week' which highlight student achievement.

- Displays demonstrating a variety of responses in different media to the same stimulus.

- Colour wheels and other informational displays, illustrating how to create perspective or use shading effectively.

- A display showing how to draw a cartoon stage by stage, using a range of different cartoon figures to highlight the process—or instructions as to how to watercolour or use other media.

- Demonstration of a design layout for an advert or webpage, with several different versions of the same topic, exhibiting different aspects of design.

- A timeline of art and artists, with velcroed pictures to try and assign to a particular period or genre at the end.

- An exploded annotation of a piece of art, demonstrating skills of commentary.

- Themed projects relating to times of year or different festivals or cultures, for instance Indian art or the art of spring.

MFL displays

- Key words are of course the lifeblood of MFL displays, and should be evident throughout—do not underrate the power of simple picture/ key word equivalent displays.

- A display of a newspaper in the target language, cut up and annotated, perhaps compared to a British paper with similar topics or on the same day.

- Magazines in the target language, used to make a display that focuses on sport or fashion, for instance.

- A problem page display in the target language—you can put the problems in English and the answers in the target language, or mix two target languages for added interest. Alternatively, put the problem in English, and offer several answers in speech bubbles with different languages, so that students have to decide which agony aunt is best.

- Use cartoon characters to illustrate common phrases—having Homer Simpson offering 'Ça va?' and Marge saying 'Bonjour' is a good way of opening out discussions about formality and informality.

Computing displays

- Using old computer components to illustrate a display of hardware makes it immediately appealing and 3D.

- A display about cyber-bullying and safety should be in every ICT room. Speech bubble questions and answers using popular celebrities, cartoon characters, or even teachers is a good way to brighten this up—students like the idea that they might know more than the headteacher about something.

- A display showing what information about you is available online, and how sites relate to each other.

- To set up IT rules, the use of Facebook 'like' and 'dislike' thumbs up and down is very effective.

- A 'tree' demonstrating programming logic in a visual way, explaining something such as how traffic lights work (could link into AFL traffic-lighting).

- An illustrated 'History of ICT' timeline is especially interesting for students who think that YouTube has always been around!

Active arts displays

Drama/performing arts displays

- A frame for a display board that looks like a stage set curtain will make pictures of recent performances look even more appealing. Similarly a cardboard proscenium arch is appealing for displays, or even above the entrance to the department.

- A diagram of a stage set, with notes illustrating how each part is decided upon—this can be matched with notes from designers commenting on different styles.

- A dance display can be linked to the contact details of local specialists in different types of dance, e.g. classical, jazz, tap, Irish.

- A lighting display, with illustrations showing the different kinds of lighting on the same person or object.

- A history of production display, demonstrating different settings and costumes for different productions of a set text.

- A costume display, for instance showing different styles of costume used for a range of productions of a given Shakespeare play.

- A programme display—either of programmes of productions that the department have taken students to see, or of those produced by the department, or a giant programme for a set text, with 'exploded' details about character, text history, and so on.

- Every drama department should have a board where local productions are highlighted. It is worth asking local amateur companies if the school can send a 'reviewer' at a reduced price.

Music displays

- 'From score to stage'—a display that shows the processes that music goes through in terms of editing, revision, processing, recording, etc.

- Orchestra display, showing where each instrument is placed, with examples of an orchestral score highlighted in different colours for the appropriate instrument.

- Timeline of instrument creation, showing how musical instruments have developed. Interesting for students who may have assumed that violins have always been around.

- World map of instrument invention and discovery, showing how different instruments have developed in different areas.

- Dissected instruments—if you have an old, broken instrument, a beguiling 3D display shows it in cross-section.

- Local concerts should be advertised and can also be reviewed in a display, to draw in a further audience. It is worth asking if the school can send a student reviewer for a reduced price.

PE/Sports Studies displays

- Animal vs human displays demonstrating how runners and jumpers in the animal kingdom compare to human athletes in terms of speed, dexterity, strength, and so on.

- A display about ball skills that has balls of different sizes stuck to the display board.

- An 'unusual sports' board that highlights sports that students may not know about. Especially good if you can link them to local teams or teachers offering that sport.

- An 'Olympic/World record' board, showing how school athletes compare to professionals. If you can, it is worth finding out early times for athletes and so on (often readily found in biographies) as your students can then claim that they are faster then Usain Bolt at the same age—or not, as the case may be.

- 'Match report' board reporting on school games, with reviews, star player awards and so on. Could also be linked to local professional or semi-professional teams—ask if students can come at a reduced price if they write up a match report.

Reflecting on the lesson

It is, of course, important that you give students time and space to reflect on what they have learned. This is part of evaluation, and one reason why a plenary is always so important. Taking student feedback about lessons into account will help you to individualise your teaching and help students progress more effectively. However, if *you* reflect on your lesson—even if it is only to think 'That was a disaster!'—then you are on your way to becoming a good teacher. Teachers who are unreflective will never improve, because they are unable to think of different ways of doing something. Considering—honestly—what went well and how it could have been better are the markers of improvement.

This is not to say that you should always be down on yourself, despairing of your ability to ever engage 11X or think of the right response to Rude year 10 Boy. As well as reflecting on what you could do better, reflect on what went well. Consider if it was worth spending all that time on that resource, or all that effort cutting up coloured squares; whether the images worked better or worse than a video. Remember that teaching is the art of the possible, and make it easier on yourself. Good teaching is not exactly lazy teaching, but it should not be exhausting and stressful either. External sources will be doing their best to ensure that you do have stress, so build in systems and structures that will make, at least, lesson planning less of an effort.

Ultimately, I've found the spider strategy saved me time and worry and ended up improving my teaching and my results; others I've shared it with have found it helpful. However if, on reflection, you want to leave something out, or think you've got a way that works better for you, then what is there to say but good luck to you, please share it, and thank you anyway.

For reading this far.

Glossary

AFL	Assessment for Learning (formative assessment strategies)
AO	Assessment Objective (specific assessment aims)
CA	Controlled Assessment
DT	Design technology
EAL	English as an Additional Language
EBI	Even Better If (points for development)
EHC	Education Health and Care plan (new form of SEN designations from September 2014)
INSET	In-Service Education and Training
IT	Information Technology
LEARN	A behaviour management system which asks students to abide by the five following rules:
	L = Listen and pay attention when the teacher is talking
	E = Bring all equipment for every lesson and arrive on time for lessons
	A = Aim high and put your best effort into your work
	R = Respect other students by not disrupting their learning
	N = Never talk over the teacher or over other students
LO	Learning Objective (the purpose of an individual lesson)
MFL	Modern foreign languages
OFSTED	Office for Standards in Education
PE	Physical education
PEE	Point, Evidence, Explain (paragraphing scaffold for students)
PEEL	Point, Evidence, Explain, Link (whole-text paragraphing scaffold for students)
PPA	Planning, Preparation and Assessment (teacher's time)
PSHE	Physical, Social, Health Education
RAG	Red, Amber, Green (trafficlighting system to show performance or student's confidence)
RE	Religious education

SA	School Action (A child identified as having learning difficulties and targeted for extra support as they are not making progress in line with their peers)
SA+	School Action Plus (The SA has not helped, and the school needs to seek advice from experts outside the school and/or provide more specialist intervention)
SEN	Special Educational Needs (A child has been identified as having specific learning needs not met by ordinary provision)
SIMS	School Information Management System
SMART	Targets which are Specific Measureable Achievable Realistic and Time defined.
SPEED	Signpost, point, example, explain, discuss/develop (paragraphing scaffold for developing extended writing)
TA	Teaching Assistant
WWW	What Went Well (points for praise)

References

Beere, J., (2012), *The Perfect OFSTED Lesson* (2nd edn.). Carmarthen: Crown House Publishing.

Bloom, B. S., (1956), *Taxonomy of Educational Objectives, Handbook I: The Cognitive Domain*. New York: David McKay Co Inc.

Bronte, E., (1847), *Wuthering Heights*. London: Penguin Classics.

Golding, W., (1954), *The Lord of the Flies*. London: Penguin Modern Classics.

Kottler, J. A. and Kottler, E., (2008), *Students Who Drive You Crazy: Succeeding With Resistant, Unmotivated, and Otherwise Difficult Young People* (2nd edn.). London: Sage.

Myhrvold, N., Young, C., and Bilet, M., (2011), *Modernist Cuisine: The Art and Science of Cooking*. New York: Barnes & Noble.

Steinbeck, J., (1937), *Of Mice and Men*. London: Penguin Modern Classics.

Index

Index